MW00526207

FAITH DRIVEN INVESTING

Contributors include Timothy Keller,
Andy Crouch, *and* Cathie Wood

FAITH
DRI>EN
Investing

Every Investment Has an Impact—<u>*What's Yours?*</u>

TYNDALE
MOMENTUM®

A Tyndale nonfiction imprint

Visit Tyndale online at tyndale.com.

Visit Tyndale Momentum online at tyndalemomentum.com.

Tyndale, Tyndale's quill logo, *Tyndale Momentum*, and the Tyndale Momentum logo are registered trademarks of Tyndale House Ministries. Tyndale Momentum is a nonfiction imprint of Tyndale House Publishers, Carol Stream, Illinois.

Certified Kingdom Advisor® and CKA® are registered trademarks of Kingdom Advisors, Inc.

Faith Driven Investing: Every Investment Has an Impact—What's Yours?

Designed by Faceout Studios, Spencer Fuller

Edited by Jonathan Schindler

All Scripture quotations, unless otherwise indicated, are taken from the Holy Bible, *New International Version*,® NIV.® Copyright © 1973, 1978, 1984, 2011 by Biblica, Inc.® Used by permission. All rights reserved worldwide.

Scripture quotations marked ESV are from The ESV® Bible (The Holy Bible, English Standard Version®), copyright © 2001 by Crossway, a publishing ministry of Good News Publishers. Used by permission. All rights reserved.

For information about special discounts for bulk purchases, please contact Tyndale House Publishers at csresponse@tyndale.com, or call 1-855-277-9400.

Library of Congress Cataloging-in-Publication Data

A catalog record for this book is available from the Library of Congress.

ISBN 978-1-4964-7446-9

Printed in the United States of America

28 27 26 25 24 23 22
7   6   5   4   3   2   1

CONTENTS

ACKNOWLEDGMENTS

From the Faith Driven Investor team

The Faith Driven Investor movement is not new. Groups of Christ-followers have long gathered together to place their investment capital in ventures that are about God's Kingdom. From the Moravians to the Guinness family and Larry Burkett to Ron Blue (just to name a few), this has been going on for hundreds of years. As a ministry, we're excited to build on the work of the leaders who have paved the way for God's redemptive work in and through capital investments.

For us, the newest phase of the Faith Driven Investor movement really began with a few dozen folks at a French bistro in Palo Alto after a Sovereign's Capital annual meeting. There were people from National Christian Foundation, TrustBridge, Praxis, Impact Foundation, and others who helped begin a conversation that spawned a movement that has led to this book.

Many of us in that group were and are investors, but we had a desire to make the movement about much more than any one fund. We shared a conviction that we weren't doing enough to call people's attention to a renewed sense of thinking; rather, we were calling people's attention to a new fund. Frankly, we were being too small-minded and self-centered.

It's because of the people in that group, however, that something changed. Almost exactly one year later, those same people plus 150 others met for the first Faith Driven Investor gathering in Park City, Utah, at the tail end of the Christian Economic Forum to understand how we might work together to advance the work of God through the work of Faith Driven Investing professionals across all different investment classes.

When we gathered, we likened the Faith Driven Investing landscape to a 1980s Russian grocery store whose shelves were devoid of product. There was a sense that faith-driven ventures simply weren't available to the public. But we also commented that, unlike a 1980s Russian grocery store, there didn't seem to be much demand for faith-driven investments either. Many people seemed to not even know that investing was something that had a faith component to it.

Fast-forward a few years, and the Faith Driven Entrepreneur and Faith Driven Investor ministries provide regular online content, an annual conference, a book (now two!), and community-building resources focused entirely on helping people understand how faith in God can impact the way we lead our businesses and manage our investment portfolios.

In a lot of ways, that first gathering seems like a distant memory. But at the same time, as we invited some of the best leaders, thinkers, and investors to help us create this book, it feels like we're back there all over again. The Faith Driven Investor movement is not new. It has been going on for centuries, if not millennia. And yet there is a new energy around Faith Driven Investing that has led to the creation of this resource.

The Faith Driven Investor team is growing. The movement is expanding beyond borders. We are so excited about what the future has in store. But none of this would've come together if it weren't for the following people.

Thanks first and foremost to God, without whom none of this—the book, the movement, the people—would exist. We owe him everything.

Thanks to the contributors to this book. The unique ways God has gifted you to lift up this movement and the selfless way you bring the body of Christ together are beautiful to watch. Thank you for sharing your stories with us through conversations and interviews that have continued to inspire us along the way. We can't wait for your words to help lead and inspire people toward the life God is calling them to.

While we wanted this book to be an ensemble project that pulled together voices of the movement, there's no way we can fit all the stories in it. We're grateful for so many who have shared their stories through podcasts, conferences, and other channels. Specifically, thanks to friends like Brian Fikkert, Randy Alcorn, Chuck Bentley, Chip Ingram, J. D. Greear, and so many other leaders and pastors who have spent a lifetime challenging us to serve God and get this area of money and assets right.

Thanks to Daryl Heald, April Chapman, Todd Harper, Emanuel Bistrian, and the teams at Generous Giving and Generosity Path who help us understand how and where we might steward capital to know God more fully and participate in the work that he is doing.

For so many friends who have lived radical generosity out and have led all of us to see the potential to unlock our investable capital to make an impact, your inspiration and trailblazing are igniting a movement.

Thanks to Jeff Johns and Aimee Minnich and the Impact Foundation, David Wills and the team at National Christian Foundation, and Bob Collins and the team at TrustBridge for pioneering the way that Christ-followers can steward investment assets with their philanthropic capital.

Thanks to the many who are building out the practical businesses that allow the body of Christ to put capital to work, from Luke Roush, John Coleman, and Jake Thomsen at Sovereign's Capital to Wes Lyons at Eagle Venture Fund for the way you invest in leaders motivated by their Christian faith. Thanks to Robin John and Jason Myhre at Eventide Asset Management for helping us understand that every investment has an impact. Thanks to Tim Macready, Rachel McDonough, Mark Wesson, and so many others that lead in the advisory spaces and public markets. A special thanks to Pete Kelly, Ben Erskine, Jimmy Song, Jon Erwin, and Dallas Jenkins for helping us to understand how Faith Driven Investing impacts more than just equities.

Thanks to those who are changing the way investing will be seen in emerging economies, including friends like Pieter Faure, Ndidi Nwuneli, Neil Holzapfel, Johan du Preez, Malcolm Johnston, Craig Shugart, Don Simmons, Matthew Rohrs, and Peter Greer.

Thanks to friends like Dave Blanchard, Luke Dooley, Chuck Welden, and Josh Kwan. Your work with ministries like Praxis, OCEAN, Lion's Den, and The Gathering inspires what it looks like for like-minded entrepreneurs and investors to come together and redeem the world around us.

Thanks to those at the center of this community and to John Siverling, who has kept the conversation growing through his faithful leadership.

Thanks to the movement's countless volunteers: the leaders of Faith Driven Investor groups and event site hosts. Your selfless sacrifice and your passion to serve reminds us all that life is better in community. The way you lead is an encouragement and a gift to us all.

This idea would also not be roaring to life today without such a dedicated team serving behind the scenes. Jonny

Wills, the gift God has given you to bring a voice and continuity to this movement is truly incredible. Thank you for your commitment to excellence and your patience to walk through this process with us. You give voice and encouragement to entrepreneurs and investors around the world.

To the humble heroes of the Faith Driven team, the way you serve so selflessly is an inspiration. The shared commitment to make this movement about God's glory among the nations is a gift to watch. It's one of life's great gifts to be on this journey together.

INTRODUCTION

Henry Kaestner

Does your faith affect the way you invest?

This question comes with an easy answer: yes! Faith affects everything. All of us are driven by our faith in one way or another. Whether it's our faith in God, our faith in the markets, our faith in our retirement plan, our faith in our ability to provide for ourselves, or any other object we place our faith in, we can safely say that we are all Faith Driven Investors.

The trickier question is this: *How* does your faith affect the way you invest?

There is a long list of sermons, articles, podcasts, and more for Christ-followers thinking through charitable giving, but there is a surprisingly short collection of resources that help Christians understand how God uses capital markets for his purposes and glory.

Charitable giving, of course, is a huge part of how God works in and through money. But we don't think charity and investing should be seen as two separate entities. Giving can be investing but with a focus on spiritual returns over financial ones. It's a mindful and intentional use of resources.

The Faith Driven Investing movement is really all about how we steward all the financial resources God has given us. It's about how the Holy Spirit moves through the faithful stewardship of capital. It's about giving. It's about investing. It's about seeing God's Kingdom come and God's will be done through all that he has entrusted to us.

Knowing that there are some great books about generosity and the stewardship of philanthropic capital available, we've focused in this book on how God might have us use investments in capital markets that come with a financial return for his glory. Welcome to the conversation.

This book is full of stories of how God's people are bringing their all to the altar. They are being transformed by the renewing of their minds. They are endeavoring to overcome the world rather than be polluted by it. And through God's power, they are overcoming the worries of the world and the deceitfulness of riches.

These are the stories of entrepreneurs, leaders, preachers, teachers, businesspeople, and professional, accredited investors. Although they come from different backgrounds, they all share a deep love for God, a desire to make his name known, and a sense that investing may have something to do with that.

This book is not a how-to guide. Instead, you'll find different viewpoints, all describing the ways that faith can and will intersect with the way we invest. What you'll find is an approach to investing that challenges the status quo.

The traditional mindset of Christ-followers is to make as much money as we possibly can in our left hand and then—to the extent that we understand the biblical message of generosity—to give away as much as we possibly can with our right hand to ministries and missions that we care about. However, the body of Christ is coming to understand that the very investment capital we have in our left hand might accomplish the same missions and ministry goals that we have in our right. But how? That's what we're exploring in this book.

We're having a conversation with the men and women who have been a part of this movement long before *Faith Driven Investor* was a podcast and a website. We're talking with Tim Keller, Cathie Wood, Andy Crouch, Finny Kuruvilla, and a dozen other wise leaders who are asking and answering many of the same questions you may have:

- What is the standard of excellence for a Christian investor?
- What does the Bible say about investing?
- How are capital markets capable of advancing the gospel around the world?

- What types of returns make for a great investment?
- How can entrepreneurs and investors experience a healthy working relationship?
- What is the role of risk in investments?
- How does an eternal mindset change the way we live, work, give, save, and invest today?

It's likely that you already have some answers in mind for each of these questions. It's also likely that your answers are different from others reading this same thing. But that's the point. It would be easy to write a book on investing focused on doing things with excellence and being a good steward. Writing a book that stays on the surface would be an easy way to get a "yes and amen!" But that doesn't necessarily advance the movement or bring clarity to our end goal.

Instead, I want to invite you into the conversations that may not have clear answers—not so that we can determine the end-all, be-all solution, but so we can join the people who are in the process of figuring it out. Our hope is that you read this book and find some of the answers you're looking for when it comes to fusing your faith and your investing. But perhaps most important, our hope is that your eyes are opened to the many ways God has chosen to work through his people.

This is about a joyous expectation that we follow a God who loves inviting his people into what he is doing throughout the world. We know that God answers prayers for healing sometimes with miracles but most often with the hard work and dedication of skilled doctors and nurses. God is still the one doing the work, but he has chosen to use the hands of people to deliver what he wants to give. This is what he's doing with our investments. God is in the business of using the things he has put in our hands to provide for and love our neighbors and the world. And he wants you to experience the joy that comes from doing so.

The church has a tendency to make gray issues black and white. Our hope isn't to prescribe what you do with your investment capital. However, we do want to prescribe a greater understanding of how God uses your investment capital. We want to encourage you to join us at the feet of an almighty God as we ask him to show us how to steward what he has given us.

The following stories are wonderful examples of men and women moving from a realization that where they allocate capital matters toward a practical understanding of how that shapes the paths they've chosen to follow. The hope is that you find encouragement in the stories themselves, as well as in the variety of ways in which a Spirit-led heart can see capital and assets as the means through which God's love and grace move throughout the world.

Every investment has an impact. What's yours?

PART 1

FAITH DRIVEN INVESTORS ARE...

CHAPTER 1

IDENTIFIED IN CHRIST

Timothy Keller

Martyn Lloyd-Jones was a Welsh Presbyterian minister who lived in the mid-twentieth century. Before leaving medicine for the ministry, he was physician to the royal family in England. Dr. Lloyd-Jones once said, "There are many whom I have had the privilege of meeting, whose tombstone might well bear the grim epitaph: '. . . born a man, died a doctor'!"[1] What he meant is that there are certain professions that become more than what you do. They become who you are. They become your identity.

Among many that could be named, one of them is business and finance.

Most Christian believers understand at some level that we need to find our identity in Christ rather than in other things. Still, the fact of the matter is, no matter where you live, every culture gives its members a way of forming an identity. The trouble is that your culture rarely tells you that's what it's doing to you. Rather, it just forces a particular process of identity formation on you, and it's almost always invisible to you.

Before we discuss how this happens, let's first define identity. Your identity, whatever it is, assumes answers to three questions:

- What am I like?
- What am I worth?
- Who gets to say?

An extremely important book in Western thought in the last generation is Charles Taylor's *Sources of the Self: The Making of the Modern Identity.* Taylor says that to make sense of our lives—to have an identity—we need an orientation to the good of something incomparably higher than us. That is, to have a sense of who we are, we must have a notion of where we have been and where we are going in relation to this good.

Another way of saying this is that everyone must live for something. You will have to make something the main thing to which you aspire, your highest good, or the thing to which you are most committed. Everybody has something that they're living for, and your identity is your connection to that thing.

I was once pastorally counseling two different women who each had an adolescent son who was beginning to misbehave in serious ways. At the same time, I was also counseling two actors in New York City, both of whom had recently received real hope that their careers were going to take off, which was quickly followed by their careers going in the tank.

In both cases, the people handled their situations very differently. One of the women with a misbehaving son was grieved but doing okay; the other one was falling apart. One actor was frustrated but surviving; the other one was falling apart. And I began to realize that there was a shared difference between them.

Though both women loved their sons, the second woman found her identity in being a good mother. That was who she was. Though both actors were passionate about their work, the one who fell apart had put his identity into his career and receiving recognition as an actor.

If you love your son and he goes off the rails, then you're heartbroken, but your sense of self isn't crushed. However, if your very identity is "I'm a great mother" and your son goes off the rails, you don't have a self left. The strange part of this is that a lot of your grief over the condition of your son is actually selfish. It's not about him. It's about you and your status as a parent.

Is this true for you and your business? Are your finances, your investing strategy, or your ingenuity truly the things holding your personhood together? If you don't know, imagine what would happen if you lost them. God tells us that he is a jealous God and prone to toppling the idols distracting his people from worshiping him. This may be the heart check you need: *What would happen if you lost it all? What would that do to your sense of self?* It's easy (and quite common) to measure our worth and value by our assets under management, return performance, Morningstar rating, or some other metric, but if your ability to invest well is your identity, you're in danger.

Another way to discern if your business is your identity is by looking at your calendar. If you're a workaholic—someone who works and works and works and *enjoys* being overworked (or worse yet, doesn't understand the meaning of *overworked*)—that might be a hint of where you're finding your identity.

Here's a different example. Years ago, my wife confronted me and said, "You know, when it comes to money, generally speaking, you're pretty disciplined." I sat up straight in my chair, enjoying where this appeared to be going . . . until she continued, "But there's one area where you just get out of control, and you don't even realize it. You spend money on books." She wasn't done. She said, "You know why? Because you get your identity from looking smart. You want people to think you're really smart, so reading books has become a part of your identity."

She was right.

I buy book after book after book because of how I define myself. Because my identity is wrapped up in that, I don't even realize what I'm doing. The same is true for work. When it becomes more than something you do—more than a means to an end—it has taken over who you are.

Another metric is the whiplash of success and failure. To put it mildly, success is wonderful. However, if it's your identity, then success really does go to your head. You become an arrogant person. One of the marks of this is a person who says, "I made a lot of money, which means I'm an expert in every area of life." The other extreme, of course, is when failure utterly destroys you to the point where you don't have a self left.

One more warning that you've misplaced your identity is if you're incapable of critiquing yourself. A man named Benjamin Nugent wrote an interesting article in the *New York Times* some years ago in which he realized that he was living for his writing. His very identity was how successful a writer he was.

What he said was that whenever somebody tried to edit him, he couldn't take it. If somebody tried to change anything, he just freaked out. Why? Because, as he said, "I made the quality of my work the measure of my worth."[2] Because his work was his worth, he couldn't handle negative feedback. It was more than a critique of his writing—it was a critique of his identity.

A relationship with Jesus Christ and an identity that flows from who he is and what he has done for us changes everything. It radically transforms the way we work, the way we invest, the way we view money, all of it. How? Here are four ways.

First, the Christian faith gives us a moral compass, an inner GPS, that provides ethical guidance that takes us beyond merely the legal aspects or requirements in any situation. A Christian on the board of a major financial institution—recently publicly embarrassed by revelations of corruption—told me about a closed-door meeting there between top executives. Someone said, "We have to restore moral values." Immediately someone asked, "Whose values? Who gets to define what is moral?" And there's our problem.

There once was a perception of broadly felt moral intuitions that governed much behavior in our society. It went well beyond the legal. Much of the ruthlessness, lack of transparency, and lack of integrity that characterizes Wall Street, the marketplace, and many other professions today comes because consensus on those moral intuitions has collapsed. However, Christians working in those worlds do have solid ethical guidance and could address through personal example the values vacuum that has now been recognized by so many.

Second, your Christian faith gives you a new spiritual power, an inner gyroscope, that keeps you from being overthrown by either success, failure, or boredom. Regarding success and failure, the gospel helps Christians find our deepest identity not in accomplishments but in who we are in Christ. This keeps our egos from inflating too much during seasons of prosperity, and it prevents bitterness and despondency during times of adversity. While some jobs seduce us into overwork and anxiety, others tempt us to surrender to drudgery, only "working for the weekend," doing just what is necessary to get by when someone is watching. Paul calls that "eye-service" (Colossians 3:22-24, ESV) and charges us to think of every job as working for God, who sees everything and loves us. That makes high-pressure jobs bearable and even the most modest work meaningful.

Third, the Christian faith gives us a new conception of work as one of the ways God loves and cares for his world—through us. Look at the places in the Bible that say God gives every person their food. How does God do that? It is through human work—from the farmhand milking the cows, to the truck driver bringing produce, to the local grocer. God could feed us directly, but he chooses to do it through human work.

There are three important implications of this. First, it means all work, even the most menial task, has great dignity.

In our work we are God's hands and fingers, sustaining and caring for his world. Further, it means one of the main ways to please God in our work is simply to do work well. This includes the farmhand we just mentioned and the green, fresh-out-of-college kid who's grinding away on Excel spreadsheets. Some have called this "the ministry of competence." What passengers need first from an airline pilot is not that she speaks to them about Jesus but that she is a great, skillful pilot. Finally, this means that Christians can and must have deep appreciation for the work of those who work skillfully but do not share our beliefs.

Fourth, the Christian faith gives us a new world-and-life view that shapes the character of our work. All well-done work that serves the good of human beings pleases God. But what exactly is "the common good"? There are many work tasks that do not require us to reflect too much on that question. All human beings need to eat, so raising and providing food serves people well. But what if you are an elementary school teacher or a playwright? What is good education (i.e., what should you be teaching children)? What kinds of plays should you write (i.e., what kinds of stories do people need)? The answers to these questions will depend largely on how you answer more fundamental questions: What is the purpose of human life? What is life about? What does a good human life look like? It is unavoidable that many jobs will be shaped by our conscious or semiconscious beliefs about those issues. So Christians must think out how their faith will distinctly shape their work.

How wonderful that the gospel works on every aspect of us—mind, will, and feelings—and enables us to both deeply appreciate the work of nonbelievers and yet aspire to work in unique ways as believers. Putting these four aspects together, we see that being a Christian leads us to see our work not as merely a way to earn money, nor as primarily a means of personal advancement, but as truly a calling—to serve God and love our neighbor.

In Luke 10:17-20, Jesus sends his disciples out to heal and to cast out demons. When they return, Jesus inquires how it went. They respond, "Wow, Lord, even the demons are subject to us!" (In other words, "We had a very successful investment year!") "It was unbelievable. We cast out demons. We trampled on serpents. We did all these things, and it was great!"

What does Jesus say to them in response? "Do not rejoice in this, that the spirits are subject to you, but rejoice that your names are written in heaven" (verse 20, ESV). That is certainly an interesting response. Surely, he doesn't mean *not* to be happy that they have changed people's lives. Why wouldn't they be happy?

Rather, Jesus is saying to them, "You're rejoicing about the wrong things. You're making these works into your identity." Similarly, there is that famous parable of the rich man and

Lazarus in Luke 16. Ironically, the rich man is never given a name. He is just "the rich man." Why? Well, that's who he was. His identity was in being a rich man. If your identity is in your riches (or in your children or in anything else other than Jesus), you actually don't have a name at all. You're just a "rich man."

What Jesus is reminding us here is that we must deliberately keep our hearts from resting in our self-created identities, in our success. The real success, Jesus says, is that because of what he has done, our names are already written in heaven. We will be received there. There is real success, real power, real riches, and it is guaranteed. Nonetheless, it takes years to get this into our hearts.

I talked to a friend some years ago who was very upset with criticism he had received that attacked his reputation. One day he was reading Philippians 2 in the old King James Version, where it says that Jesus Christ, though he was "equal with God," "made himself of no reputation" (see verses 6-7). And suddenly the beauty of it struck his heart. He told me, "I got a new freedom because I suddenly realized Jesus became small so that I could have a name that lasted forever. He lost everything so I could be brought in." He never had the same problem with criticism after that.

Why do you pray? Why do you worship? Why do you take the Lord's Supper? Why do you do devotions? Because you're working this identity more and more into yourself. It's not all the way in there—and it will never be in this life—but keep it up, because it is your true freedom.

Rejoice, not that you've had a great year with profitable investments, nor that you've made the Midas List and were mentioned in the *Financial Times*, but that your name is written in heaven. This is the beginning. This is the foundation upon which you can build your investment strategy, your business practice, and your life. Start now.

CHAPTER 2

THE SERVANT OF ONE MASTER

Andy Crouch

There are two mysteries relating to Jesus' most famous words about money. You're probably already familiar with them: "You cannot serve God and money" (Matthew 6:24, ESV). One mystery actually relates to the proper translation of that last word, but let's start with the other mystery, which can be put very simply: Why not?

Why *can't* you serve God and money, each in their appropriate way—the way Jesus said you could serve God and Caesar? Caesar, of course, was the pagan emperor of the Roman Empire. At the time of Jesus, the Jewish people questioned whether they should even pay taxes to Caesar. But

Jesus said, "Render to Caesar the things that are Caesar's, and to God the things that are God's" (Matthew 22:21, ESV). In other words, he encouraged people to serve Caesar in the way proper to Caesar. To be sure, we should not serve Caesar the way we serve God. But the plain meaning of Jesus' words is that it is possible to serve Caesar, in some sense, and to serve God as well.

This reads so differently from the way Jesus talks about money. We can serve God and Caesar, but we can't serve God and money. Why? Why is money more powerful than Caesar? I want to suggest it's because money, especially in large quantities, gives you a power that Caesar does not have.

WHAT IS MONEY?

You probably learned the defining qualities of money in economics. Money is a medium of exchange, a unit of account, and a store of value. Or to put it another way, money is fungible, countable, and storable. It is also, more fundamentally, a form of power. Power is the ability to get things done in the world, or the ability to get what you want, regardless of whether that thing or that desire is shared by other people. Money gives you a form of power that's fungible, countable, and storable. And it turns out that these distinctive qualities make money a most unusual form of power.

Money is *fungible*. This is a key distinction between most forms of power and money. Money is of very little use all by itself, but you can turn it into whatever you want. That's not true of most forms of power, including Caesar's. Caesar had a great deal of power as the lord of the Roman Empire, but he could only exercise his power in that office in that land. He couldn't arbitrarily decide he wanted something totally different from the rule of the empire, let alone exercise his power somewhere else. Military or political power like Caesar's is contextual, limited to a particular function and place.

This is not so true of money. Money allows you to use power anywhere that legal tender is accepted. You can exchange it into anything. That's a kind of power that Caesar didn't know, at least not in his role as emperor.

Money is *countable*. You know exactly how much of it you have, whereas that isn't always so clear with other forms of power.

How much power does the CEO of a company have? Certainly some, perhaps a great deal. But if you've ever been in that role, you know that it's hard to know exactly how much. There's certainly no way to count it. But you can measure money, you can count money, you can know exactly how much is on your balance sheet and how much is available to spend. Most power comes with significant uncertainty about its amount and extent, but with money that is all quite clear.

The final differentiator is that money is *storable*. You can save it for later. Most power has to be exercised precisely at the moment when you have it. As a public speaker, I speak to audiences of people, sometimes large audiences, at particular places and times. That's certainly a form of power. But if I were to show up on the day I'm scheduled to speak and ask to save that power for later, it's unlikely anyone would stick around. Power is almost always bound to a certain time or place. But if I have money, I can use it at the time of my choosing. That, too, is a kind of power that Caesar didn't have.

All of these factors add up to power that is independent. Political and military rule are, in meaningful ways, forms of power that are dependent. Caesar, like other Roman emperors, only had his power because he was the adopted son of a powerful man. That relationship gave him power. Even in our modern democracies, people are granted power—almost always for a limited time—by the consent of the governed.

But if you have enough money, the honest truth is you can get almost anything done you want without anyone really having to know or care or possibly even validate who you are—because money talks without you needing to be known, let alone loved. It's impersonal power. This is a power greater than any other in the world.

And if you have this kind of power, or can imagine having it, why would you need God? When you can get what you want, whatever you want, when you want it—when you know how much you have, you can store it, and you don't

THE SERVANT OF ONE MASTER

have to be any particular kind of person to use it—who needs God?

This is the fundamental reason that serving God and serving money are incompatible. The type of power that money affords is the most direct rival to God in human affairs. And the reason money is such a fantasy- and anxiety-inducing substance, the reason it keeps us up at night and always makes us desperate for more, is because of the kind of power we imagine it will give us.

MONEY AND MAMMON

We've begun to understand why Jesus teaches differently about Caesar and money. We can serve God and Caesar, but we can't serve God and money. But there's also something deeper going on, and it involves the particular word that Jesus used.

Though the Gospels are written in Greek, it's likely that Jesus spoke Aramaic, the common language of Judea, his whole life. His biographers, the Gospel writers, translated his words into the language their own readers understood, which we in turn translate into English. But every once in a while, the Gospels leave an Aramaic word untranslated, and they do so in this case. They write down, in Greek, "You cannot serve God and *Mammon*." That last word is not translated, but simply transliterated from the Aramaic—a Semitic word that roughly means money or assets held in trust.

What does it mean that we can't serve, not just God and money, but God and Mammon? Why is that word left untranslated?

One explanation is to look at other words the Gospel writers, and translators in general, leave untranslated. Mostly they are names, or what grammarians call proper nouns. We generally don't translate a name from one language to another—at best, we transliterate it to make it easier to pronounce (in fact, we do this with the Hebrew name *Yeshua*, which means "God rescues" but which we render in English as *Jesus*).

Transliteration, not translation, is what the Gospel writers do with Jesus' word *mammon*, and the early church concluded that the reason they did this is because the Gospel writers understood that Jesus was not using the word as a common noun. He was not even just speaking of a principle or an idea. He was—the early church came to believe—using the word as a quasi-personal name.

Mammon, the early church concluded, was not just an idea or a principle but the name of a being in service of the enemy of all that is good. Mammon is an opponent of all God's works in the world, a servant of the ultimate opponent of God, the one Jesus called Satan or the devil. Mammon is a demonic force at work in history, with a quasi-personal ability to whisper and speak to human beings and a will to distort human affairs in a particular direction.

Another way to think of this is that Mammon represents the quest to make something happen in the world apart from God. Mammon's will is the opposite of God's will. God made a good, beautiful, abundant material world. He filled it with people. He said that the world was very good, and he instructed humanity, in loving dependence on him, to subdue the earth, multiply, and bring forth all the possibility and value inherent in the created world. God's will is for the world to fill with people, people who will become full of the knowledge and love of God, full of the knowledge and love of one another, and in some ways, full of the knowledge and love of the world itself.

Again, Mammon's will is the exact opposite of God's. Mammon hates God. It wants us never to depend on God. Mammon hates creation itself. Mammon wants to destroy the earth and all that's in it, replacing the material with the immaterial, the physical with the merely spiritual, the power of love with the pride of self. And of course, Mammon hates all that is personal—especially people who are dependent on God, interdependent with one another, and guided by love.

And indeed, the story of money tracks, to an alarming degree, with the will of Mammon. As money has become more advanced, it has become less and less physical—from gold to currency to mere symbols, numbers that we track in our minds and accounting systems. All this serves the desires of Mammon perfectly.

Mammon wants the world to operate impersonally. It wants to turn even people into things. In fact, once Mammon really gets its grip on a human society, as it had gotten its grip on the Roman Empire, as it got its grip on the capitalism that built our Western world, the result is treating people impersonally.

This is, after all, the definition of slavery. Slavery is treating a person like property, treating a person like a thing. And while God wants the world to be filled with people so that the whole world will be known and loved and God will be known and loved, Mammon wants to empty the world of people and make everything feel impersonal.

No wonder Jesus says you cannot serve these two fundamentally opposed forces in the world.

You cannot serve a demon that wants to destroy a person's relationship to creation and also serve the true God who wants to reunite people, restore relationships, and liberate creation from its bondage to decay. You cannot serve God and Mammon.

What does it mean, then, to be a Faith Driven Investor? Investing focuses on the deployment of many kinds of resources, but especially financial ones, to have some sort of generative impact or influence in the world. Is our job simply to do that with broadly Christian principles? Is our calling simply to apply certain minimal ethical standards to the way we use money? I would argue that is not nearly deep enough for what we're actually called to do.

Faith Driven Investors are meant to be people who operate in close proximity to money, and thus within earshot of the whisperings and power of Mammon, with the goal of taking back territory from this demonic force and its false promises of fungible, countable, storable power. The mission of such men and women is to reclaim territory for the relational, creation-loving God who has placed us here to tend his world.

To do that we will need a twofold plan—a plan to defeat Mammon on its own territory and to reclaim what is rightfully God's through creative resistance.

DETHRONING MAMMON

Here are two quick ideas for how to "detox" from the power of Mammon in our lives.

The first and most basic way to dethrone money and Mammon is generosity—giving. Most of the ways we use money are designed to deliver some measure of control and safety. But giving, by definition, *releases* control. When you give, you're giving up a store of value that you could have held on to for some other use. Giving is the most basic detox from Mammon you can find.

The Christian church has often taught the principle of tithing on income, which is great. What has been transformative for my own life, however, that I encourage others to consider, is tithing not just on income but on assets. Our family has done this twice in the last ten years—calculated our net worth and then developed a plan to give away at least 10 percent of the total. If you've never tried this, it's incredibly hard to pull the trigger. Your assets are a store for the future, so it feels scary to give up even a small piece of optionality—all that fungible, countable, stored power. But the joy and freedom that results from tithing on assets, in our experience, is unmatched. That's what God wants to give his people. He wants to free us from the burden of Mammon. Generous giving is the simplest way to ensure that money doesn't have undue influence over us.

The second detox move is transparency. This idea meets far more resistance, for some reason, than generosity. But in my view, the secrecy we maintain about our income, our assets, and our liabilities is a sign of how powerfully the empire of Mammon has its grip on us. There is no more powerful way to release that grip than to open up our personal financial books to others.

Of course, this should be done with discretion, and it's up to you to determine what this may look like in your life and whom you trust, but in my life being open about our family's income, spending, saving, giving, and net worth—using the current actual figures—has been a game changer. Though I don't share this information in a totally indiscriminate way—on the Internet or, for that matter, in a book chapter like this—in almost any conversation where the information is relevant, I gladly and proactively talk about our family's financial situation with real numbers. I do the same when I'm asked to speak on topics relating to money or generosity—which has prompted countless people to tell me that I am literally the first Christian they have ever met who has told them how much money I earn and am responsible for stewarding.

This should not be. In every other area of our lives, we know the great benefits of opening ourselves up to those we trust. Why should money be any different? Money, after all, is something God has entrusted to us, as members of his redemptive community. It's our responsibility to handle it accordingly. In no other area do faithful Christians imagine that we can handle both opportunity and temptation entirely on our own. In the context of our shared responsibility to steward our assets for the common good, the impulse to hide what we have (and what we owe) is very likely a symptom of trying to serve God and money.

But suppose we detoxed from this impulse—if we became routinely, lavishly generous and routinely, freely open about what resources have been entrusted to us. Think of what we could be free to do.

CREATIVE RESISTANCE TO MAMMON

It is good to detox from Mammon, but let's look at other ways to offer creative resistance to this force. The very best place to start is by prioritizing people. In every transaction, every investment, every business decision, how can we prioritize people over money?

When we prioritize people, the primary question we will ask about every deployment of our assets—including our spending, saving, investing, and giving—is: What will this do to strengthen my relationships and create a deeper capacity of love and dignity and respect for others? That is, after all, what God calls his people to do. Only those who are free of Mammon will see every transaction as an opportunity for love. When we prioritize people, we're telling them that we love, honor, and respect them—exactly counter to what Mammon would have us do.

The second strategy of creative resistance to Mammon is patience. Mammon, at its core, is in a hurry. Mammon wants you to make more money and make it faster. Mammon wants you to move so quickly you don't notice the people you're running over along the way. Thankfully, the Holy Spirit within us makes available to us the incredible divine patience that Jesus showed throughout his life. We don't have to be in a hurry.

God wants us to be in the world to create multiples on our investments, for sure. But the timing, the velocity, how fast money moves is ultimately up to God.

This attitude will lead us to have a thousand-generation vision for our lives.

If you give yourself over to Mammon—if you act in all the exploitative ways Mammon would have you act in order to get more of that fungible, countable, storable power—you will do a lot of damage. But we know how long that damage will last. God says that if we enter into that kind of iniquity, it will do damage "to the third and fourth generation" (Deuteronomy 5:9, ESV).

But the interesting thing is that, even if we operate quite ethically, according to the principles we are taught in modern investing and business best practices, the results of even our best investments will most likely last three or four generations at best.

Look at family wealth. The reality is that most family wealth is exhausted after three or four generations. Few businesses last longer than three or four generations. Most of the work you and I do on a daily basis, let alone the financial investments we make, is only realistically going to have a perceptible effect—even if we are very diligent and fortunate—for three or four generations.

Yet God says, to those who love him and keep his commands and walk in his ways, he will bestow blessing to the thousandth generation.[1] That's what happens when you serve God instead of Mammon. The thousandth generation.

That type of investment won't be measured in financial return alone. Instead, it will advance the flourishing of persons and the transmission of love. It will create redemptive possibility in the world. And this kind of investment is only possible when we are completely serving God, when we've completely detoxed from serving money.

Can we do this? Can we live in this world that Mammon rules in a totally different way? Can we totally dethrone its power from our lives so that every worker, investor, spender, saver, and giver is devoted to God and God's ways? Can we prioritize people and pursue patience?

It's as easy as a camel going through the eye of a needle, isn't it?

With human beings, it's impossible. But with God, all things are possible.

CHAPTER 3

ATTUNED TO GOD'S WORD

Obie McKenzie

I fell in love with finance at Harvard Business School. Having grown up in a family of sharecroppers from West Tennessee, the campus at Cambridge felt like an entirely new world, which may in part explain why I found it so engaging. We didn't have much money growing up, which only increased my desire to study capitalism and wealth creation.

In 1972, I graduated and became the second African American hired in the business department at Morgan Stanley. I started my financial life in that bullpen, working long nights on spreadsheets that caused my eyes to blur and wound up in the trash the next morning if the senior partner found so much as a rounding error anywhere.

They were challenging days, but it's a time in my life that I'm grateful for because it has shaped the way I view life and money. I've long since benefited from the discipline that was drilled into me at Morgan Stanley. That attitude followed me as I moved from Citibank International to McKinsey & Company to Merrill Lynch to Chase to BlackRock to where I am today. After spending eighteen years at BlackRock, where the teams during my tenure raised over $30 billion of institutional assets to be managed across a number of asset classes, retirement seemed like the logical next step.

Of course, those who know me best knew that wouldn't happen. My work now is primarily focused on sharing the things I wish I had known at the beginning. I've learned a lot at the intersection of biblical theology and business, and I'm now hoping to share that information with the men and women who are coming behind me—the Faith Driven Investors of tomorrow.

IT STARTED WITH 2,300 BIBLE VERSES

In the richest country in the world, the top one percent of the population enjoys more wealth than the bottom 90 percent. Student debt exceeds $1 trillion, household credit card debt is around $1 trillion, and around two-thirds of US citizens live from paycheck to paycheck. The US balance sheet has over $28 trillion of debt currently, and it is growing at an unsustainable rate, as noted by the fact that the US dollar has lost over 96 percent of its purchasing power since 1913, when the Federal Reserve Act was signed by Woodrow Wilson.

Like the US government, I have spent so many years spending money I really don't have, to buy things I really don't need, to impress people who really don't care, only to discover that the Bible offers me a better way to live.

It was through work with Crown Financial Ministries that I first learned the Bible contains more than 2,300 verses that deal with money. Jesus talks about money in eleven of his thirty-nine parables. This topic matters to God.

So I started reading my Bible more. I started expositing these verses on money as I tried to discern what they meant for the Christian life, what they meant for *my* life. Then I started talking about these verses in church. I started teaching. Since I worked in an environment that was all about money, I felt like God had put these verses in the Bible specifically for me and for the other believers whose lives were driven by finance. It didn't seem like people were talking about this topic from the stage, so I set about doing it myself.

As I meditated on the Word of God and what God had to say about money, it didn't take long to learn that there's a difference between believing God's Word in my head and believing God's Word in my heart. It's this gap that Faith Driven Investors are called to close. We know that what comes out of our mouths (and often what comes out of our wallets) reflects what's in our hearts. What we say becomes what we do, what we do becomes a habit, our habits become our character, and our character becomes our destiny.

When it comes to what the Bible has to say about money, it's easy to know the right answers in our heads. The problem is that if the idea of being able to serve only God or money is just a theory, it's only a matter of time before we put it to the test. If we believe, however, that God's Word is true and from God, then there are no hypotheticals here. What he says in the Bible is what we're called to live by.

We can't talk about biblical economics until we've allowed this truth to sink into our lives. The Bible is God-breathed. It's good for instruction and direction. It speaks to what we need to know. And it says a lot about the components of what I think is a perfect investment plan.

THE BIBLE'S INVESTMENT PLAN

Invest in God's Word first. Invest in God's work second.

That's what the Bible says about Faith Driven Investing. The combination of investing in God's Word and his work will yield God's wealth, which is eternal. This is the core of biblical economics.

We have to start by understanding that "the earth is the LORD's, and everything in it" (Psalm 24:1). Everything in it belongs to him, and that includes us. We are a part of his creation.

Many of us have gotten things twisted when it comes to money. Instead of using money to help people, many of us have chosen to use people to make money, without consideration for what God has to say about this in his written Word, the Bible. The truth that would save so many of us from the money stresses we experience stays hidden before our eyes when we don't read the Bible.

If we belong to God, and if the earth and all that's in it belong to him, then he ought to have something to say about what to do with all this stuff. Yet that's where we go wrong. We turn to the Bible and wonder what it says about what God has given us. *How do I invest? How do I make money biblically? How do I manage my assets wisely?* These are all great questions, but they're pointed at the wrong subject.

Instead, we must do as Jesus instructs us: "Seek first his kingdom and his righteousness, and all these things will be given to you as well" (Matthew 6:33). We've got it backward. We seek the stuff before we seek God. Jesus tells us of the countercultural relationship between our economy and God's economy. Our economy is motivated by self-interest, but God's economy is motivated by love. The objective of God's economy is an abundant life in the here and now and eternal life hereafter. Both economies pursue a contented life, but only one gets you there.

The goal is the same, but the first step is completely different. That's what Jesus is telling us in Matthew: "Seek first."

Seek first. What are you seeking first? Is it your interest, your concerns, your plans? Even if we're seeking to do good by God, a lot of times we're doing that because we care about the ways our actions reflect on us. We may say we're seeking God, but we're really only doing that as a means of seeking our own gain.

That's the first way to misread this passage and misunderstand the biblical economy. If we view this verse as an "if, then" promise—"If I do this, then God will give me this"— we're missing Jesus' message. Because if we're seeking the Kingdom of God solely because we want the benefit on the back end, then we're not really seeking the Kingdom of God in the first place. We're seeking our own kingdom in disguise.

Satan is here to kill, steal, and destroy.[1] That's his job on earth every single day. And the place he does that best is in your mind. That's where he works. When we think of Matthew 6:33, all the enemy wants you to do is slightly twist that verse to make it self-serving, and he's got you right where he wants you. He has an uncanny ability to take what God has intended for good and turn it just a little bit to lead to our own demise.

That's why God outlined his armor for us.[2] The helmet of salvation is there to guard your thoughts. The breastplate of righteousness is there to protect your heart. And the sword of the Spirit, the Word of God, is there to give you something to fight back with.

If you aren't sure it's important to take God's Word with you every day, consider what Jesus did when he was in the wilderness for forty days and forty nights. He was exposed, he was hungry, he was vulnerable. And every time Satan spoke to him, he fought back with the words of God. He knew what was true even when Satan's temptations made discernment difficult.

What is our response when we're tempted by opportunities to make some quick and easy cash? Are we wary of our own desires? Are we using God's Word to test ourselves, to know what God's perfect and pleasing will is?[3] If Jesus chose to dwell on God's Word, which protected him in his most vulnerable state, then so should we.

PREPARING FOR THE FUTURE

I'm encouraged by the fact that Abraham was seventy-five when God told him to leave his familiar surroundings in Harran and go to a strange land where he would become a blessing to many nations. In this stage of my life, it's my hope to use my fifty years of Wall Street experiences and my thirty years of being a student of what the Bible has to say about money to bless the next generation.

When it comes to money, there are more than enough questions. The questions of how to make it, pay bills with it, invest it, save it, and even have enough of it to retire occupy an inordinate amount of our thinking every day. The pitfalls of loving money more than loving God are illuminated by Jesus' answer when asked what the greatest commandment is. His answer was to "love the Lord your God with all your heart and with all your soul and with all your mind" (Matthew 22:37). He knew that, as Paul reminds us in 1 Timothy 6:10, "the love of money" would be the "root of all kinds of evil," so he changed the priorities of our thinking from a focus on the accumulation of stuff to a focus on him from whom all blessings flow.

Love for God begins when we communicate with him. Reading the Bible is important, but so is prayer, which is the physical conversation between God and people. I wish I had known when I was younger that I could prayerfully ask God for anything. Once I came to believe in the reality of Jesus Christ as the Son of God, this truth changed my entire worldview. By letting the words of the Bible reside in me and by allowing my heart to believe in the reality of Jesus Christ by faith, I can ask for anything. I can talk to him about anything.

Once we confess the reality of Jesus Christ with our mouths and believe that reality in our hearts (Romans 10:9), all we have to do is ask in line with his words expressed in the Bible. Like so many of us, I rarely asked God what I should do or for help when I didn't know what the next step forward looked like. I ignored the omniscient, all-knowing God who loves me and wants to care for me.

Isn't it ironic that the whole world belongs to God, yet so often we don't bother to ask him how he wants us to invest, give, spend, and save? Isn't it also ironic that the centerpiece for God's economic plan for us is to give and not to get? God is a giving God. "God so loved the world that he *gave*" (John 3:16). That's what he does. That's who he is.

When we spend time with him through his Word and through prayer, we get to experience all that he is—his love, his grace, his generosity. And that bleeds into our lives, into our jobs, into our relationships, into what we do with money, into how we invest.

That's the life of a Faith Driven Investor. That's the life of someone who is grounded in God's Word and capable of spending time on their knees in prayer, asking the Creator of everything and Savior of humanity what he would have us do. We can approach his throne knowing that if we ask, he will answer. So, why not ask?

I humbly encourage you to consider this truth. So many of us are striving to wind up with more cash in our wallets, a larger 401k, and a better-performing stock portfolio, only to end up discontented. Jesus offers us more. He came into the world so that we might have life and have it abundantly.[4] We are encouraged to seek first the kingdom of God and his righteousness and to trust that, as a result, "all these things" will be added to us by faith.

Search the Scriptures, and you will find the truth for your

abundant life. Having a solid financial life begins with accepting the reality that everything in your life belongs to God. In order to experience a functioning, biblical investment strategy, start by asking God to align your motives with his.

All the budgeting, saving, investing, and giving can come together in a plan that lines up with the directives you personally receive from God after having asked him that all-important first question: "What shall I do with what you've given me?"

He answers those who ask.

CHAPTER 4

AWARE OF THE POWER OF MONEY AND MARKETS

Finny Kuruvilla

Legend has it that as Benjamin Franklin walked out of Independence Hall following the Constitutional Convention of 1787, a woman shouted, "Doctor, what have we got? A republic or a monarchy?" To which Franklin replied, "A republic, if you can keep it."

The structure of a republic meant that the people would have the power to elect their own leaders as opposed to society sitting under the rule of an unelected monarch with limitless power. The enormous power once concentrated in the hands of the elite was now decentralized and placed in the hands of the people. And so, Franklin's response to the woman outside of Independence Hall raises the question: What will you do with this power?

Nearly two hundred years prior to the formation of the American Republic, a similarly significant shift in power took place within the finance industry in Europe in 1602.

From early civilizations and empires, the ability to develop innovations that would progress society depended heavily upon funding. Traditionally, though, funding was only available from the rulers of society who had personal wealth and the ability to tax citizens, meaning that the decisions of which innovations would succeed were made by an elite ruling class. This system prevailed during the age of exploration as voyagers sought funding for their expensive expeditions, which brings us to the very famous voyage of Christopher Columbus.

Transoceanic sailing was risky and expensive. Columbus knew he needed investors to supply the capital for such an endeavor, so he traveled around Europe looking for investors. In 1492, after failing to secure funding from John II of Portugal and Henry VII of England, Christopher Columbus entered an investment agreement with King Ferdinand and Queen Isabella of Spain, which allowed him to receive a portion of future revenues from any of the lands he claimed for Spain on his voyage. He also retained the option to invest in one-eighth of future commercial businesses that came from his explorations. For Columbus, this was very much a business proposition. But his investors would drive much influence through this business channel. Indeed, regardless of the ethical considerations of global expansion, the implications for language, culture, worldviews, and religion are difficult to overstate. Today the majority of Central and South Americans are Catholic and speak Spanish because of this arrangement.

But let's consider an alternative narrative.

What if Columbus secured French investors? Central and South America today would be French-speaking and have a very different culture. What if Columbus secured British investors? Central and South America would be English-speaking and Protestant, not Catholic. Think of the hundreds of millions of people affected by this small group of investors and explorers. These investors who backed Columbus changed the world.

HOW BUSINESS SHAPES THE GLOBE

Changing the world isn't about platitudes or kind sentiments. It's an abstract idea, yes, but there are tangible, practical strategies rooted in sound principles that can turn this concept into a reality.

While Christopher Columbus sought the favor of monarchs to fund his voyage, it wasn't until much later that an entirely new system of investing emerged in Europe. Up until the 1600s, markets existed for the public to exchange goods and services. But in 1602, for the first time, a market was created for ordinary people to buy and sell ownership in a company.

A group of merchants in Amsterdam were looking to extend their trade routes farther east and needed significant capital to fund their expansion. Rather than seek funding from the royal elite, portions of ownership in their company—the Dutch East India Trading Company—were sold to the general public. This event initiated a revolutionary relocation of power out of the hands of the ruling class and into the hands of ordinary people, allowing them to decide collectively which innovative businesses they would fund.

The power of investing had been democratized. But what does this have to do with changing the world? In short, everything. Where kings and queens were once the only ones determining what innovations and ventures received funding, a democratic market put power into the hands of the people. This shift in power, however, does not necessarily mean that world change happens because of autonomous individuals.

In his book *To Change the World*, sociologist James Davison Hunter makes a compelling argument that the real power to change the world lies with institutions. Hunter breaks down the myth of the heroic individual—the idea that individuals have the capacity and the ability to change the world—and persuasively argues and demonstrates that the real power is, in fact, within institutions.

This reality puts the onus on businesses to act, build, create, produce, and operate with the greater good in mind if the world is to change for the better. Of course, we know that businesses have not always acted responsibly. As early as 1697, *Robinson Crusoe* author and trader Daniel Defoe noted some unintended consequences to the market shift of 1602:

> [Investing has] raised the fancies of credulous people to such a height that, merely on the shadow of expectation, they have formed companies, chose committees, appointed officers, shares, and books, raised great stocks, and cried up an empty notion to that degree that people have been betrayed to part with their money for shares in a new nothing.[1]

As Defoe points out, an underlying consequence of business entities being financed by uninvolved investors was that business owners no longer felt a sense of responsibility for the actions of their businesses. And so, he opined, "When the [investors] have carried on the jest till they have sold all their own interest, they leave the cloud to vanish of itself."[2] This problem left a societal conundrum. If businesses were taking on an increasing role in shaping the culture of society, who was responsible for shaping businesses?

INVESTORS AS CHANGE AGENTS

As James Davison Hunter explains, virtually all of the great change movements that we've seen in the last several hundred years in the West have been the result of institutions. The Gilded Age that followed the Civil War in America reinforced the authority of businesses over culture as the oil, railroad, and steel industries came to dominate the economy and the American way of life.

Beyond just their products, businesses impacted the culture through the way they operated. Henry Ford's greatest impact, for example, was not the invention of the automobile—that had already been done. Rather, it was the implementation of the assembly line into the Model T manufacturing process so that automobiles could be made more quickly and less expensively.

Processes like the assembly line made it easier for corporations to grow internationally, expanding their influence to areas outside their immediate communities. In 1913, for example, General Motors established a subsidiary company in South Africa, and they began assembling vehicles in Port Elizabeth in 1926. Almost fifty years later, as America was experiencing the fruit of the Civil Rights movement, an African American Baptist minister named Leon Sullivan was appointed as a board member of General Motors, making him the company's first Black director.

The conundrum of who is responsible for shaping businesses came into greater light in 1971, when a group of Episcopalian investors who were shareholders of GM brought a shareholder resolution to the board that addressed the inhumanity of apartheid in South Africa. Sullivan advocated for the Episcopalians and aggressively urged change, not just from General Motors but from all American corporations who had interests in South Africa.

College students also fueled the fire by pressuring their universities to divest from their stock positions in companies that had operations in South Africa. In 1977, Leon Sullivan authored a set of principles mandating the equal and fair treatment of all employees in an integrated environment. These principles served as tangible standards that corporations could formally agree to as they continued to operate in South Africa. Subsequently, pressure from institutional investors mounted on some of America's largest corporations to adopt Sullivan's principles or remove operations from South Africa altogether.

During this time, activist Adele Simmons, upon becoming president of Hampshire College in 1977, urged the college's board of trustees to divest all the college's assets that were invested in companies doing business in South Africa. Writing in the *Chicago Tribune* in 2013, she retells the impact of her initial plea to the board:

By 1988, 155 universities had divested, and the
dollars were significant. In 1986, the University of
California divested, selling $3.1 billion worth of
stock. Some schools, like the University of Chicago
and Northwestern University, did not divest, at least
not totally. But faith organizations, unions, cities,
counties and states joined in. Investment funds
started to take a careful look at companies in their
portfolios that had South African ties.[3]

She recalls meeting Nelson Mandela in 1990:

He said that divestment was a crucial factor in
ending apartheid. The movement against apartheid
was led by South Africans, and Mandela was an
inspiration throughout the decades, but the actions
of U.S. investors gave the movement both visibility
and legitimacy and had a decisive economic impact.[4]

Investors, then, had an unquestionable impact on the
fall of apartheid, which officially took place in 1994. The
small group of Episcopalian investors who proposed the initial resolution to GM in 1971 took responsibility for the
power entrusted to them as investors and decided to use that
power to promote the common good, fighting an evil that
undermined human dignity. Indeed, the power of investing

applied to promoting the common good changed the lives of millions in South Africa.

Think of the problems we face today—lack of access to clean water, air pollution, mental illnesses, cancer, infectious diseases like coronaviruses, cyber theft—all of which could be helped by institutions, specifically virtuous businesses and strong churches.

If you really want to change the world, then you have to be able to change institutions. And who better to do that than Faith Driven Investors?

ACCEPTING THE RESPONSIBILITY OF INFLUENCE

Certain institutions have concentrated power to shape hearts, attitudes, and beliefs. Consider the modern multinational corporation, for example. How much have Google, Facebook, and Nike changed our habits, desires, and even our vocabulary?

These companies were funded by venture investors as well as public investors who changed the world through the movement of capital. So, as investors, the questions we need to ask ourselves are: Do we know what we own? Do we know how we're stewarding the influence our investments have afforded us?

Most of us, if we think about it, would agree that investing has long been divorced from this original and most basic purpose of simply supplying capital to support businesses. Instead, we see that most investors are trying to profit from the market rather than from any productive and intrinsic value of the underlying company. People often forget that the market consists of these underlying companies.

This distancing between the investor and the companies they own has partly been driven by things like ETFs or index funds, where you buy the entire market. Low-cost, low-fee products are prioritized. People aren't even thinking about what it is that they're owning because they're buying everything. Thus, we can say that most people *don't* know what they own. In fact, if you ask most individual investors if they know what they own, they're likely to respond that they have no idea what they own. Sadly, many financial advisors would say the same.

As Christians, we have a different mandate. By becoming an owner of a company or a business, which is what investing is, you are sanctioning and benefiting from the company's activities and practices. And this ownership confers an ethical responsibility to the investor for the activities and practices of the company. Since investing has long been divorced from its original and basic purpose—supplying capital to support businesses—investors have forfeited the power to change the world using their hard-earned capital.

As Benjamin Franklin walked out of Independence Hall that day in 1787, he knew the weight of what had been accomplished by the Constitutional Convention. The well-being of the republic now rested in the hands of the people. And he knew that the young, fragile nation would only succeed if the people recognized and accepted the responsibility.

In a similar way, the systemic shift toward democratizing investing in Amsterdam in 1602 forever changed the landscape of business. Ordinary people are now responsible for leveraging the power generated by the force of investing. But investing for the common good will only succeed if the people recognize and accept the responsibility.

In response to modern investing, which often distances investors from the companies they own and makes their responsibilities less apparent, we need to recapture the original purpose of investing by asking questions like:

- What types of companies do I want to own?
- What is the true purpose of business?
- What is my role as an investor to promote the common good?

Some have asked if exploring these questions is antithetical to a successful investment strategy. We believe the opposite is true—that these questions can be the foundation for a successful investment strategy.

The questions above undergird the ideologies of some of the most influential investors, many of whom hold a deep understanding of their responsibility. And this same invitation to participate in the fruits of investing as well as become a change agent is extended to every investor.

The question, then, is simple: What will you do with this power?

CHAPTER 5

KNOWN FOR WHAT THEY'RE FOR

Luke Roush

The Old Testament contains a lot of rules and regulations. Exodus, Leviticus, Numbers, and Deuteronomy contain an estimated 613 laws: the Ten Commandments; food laws for how to store and cook food; moral laws about murder and theft; and miscellaneous instructions about sin offerings, first fruits, constructing altars, and even future events.

The US tax code contains 2,652 pages of laws, not including the estimated 70,000 pages of provisions and additional resources. That's an estimated 35,000,000 words, or like reading the entire Bible around fifty times. But a law is just symbolic until it is enforced. In North Carolina, the game of

Bingo cannot be longer than five hours. In Louisiana, it is a crime to send someone a pizza without their knowledge. In Vermont, women must get permission from their husbands to wear false teeth. I'm pretty sure those laws are not being enforced.

Something interesting happened with the Old Testament's 613 laws. A group of people formed with a focus on laws—the Pharisees. The Pharisees felt themselves to be superior in their understanding of the law and worked hard to create a culture where strict observance of the traditional and written law was expected. Not wanting to come close to disobedience, the Pharisees came up with the idea of adding additional laws on top of these laws as a further safeguard to prevent breaking the original laws. Imagine seeing a fence near the edge of a cliff and thinking, "Let's build another fence, further back from that fence, to make sure no one goes over the edge." That's exactly what the Pharisees did.

They set up new instructions and, in effect, built a hedge around the law—like a wall around a wall. For example, one of the Ten Commandments instructs the Israelites to keep the Sabbath holy. Fair enough. One law for one day (and it's an important one!). The Pharisees, however, took it a step further. If keeping the Sabbath holy means not working during that twenty-four-hour period, they reasoned, it'd be helpful to define what qualifies as work.

The Jewish scholars then created separate categories defining what "work" meant. Hundreds of rules filled each of these categories, including restrictions on how many steps you could take, how many letters you could write, and—the one that Jesus and his disciples appeared indifferent to—how much grain you could gather (the answer is zero). Also, they decided to extend the twenty-four-hour period to twenty-five hours, just in case.

It's important to note what exactly Jesus was critical of when it came to the Pharisees. It was not their adherence to the law or their efforts toward obedience that bothered him. It's that they had taken what God meant for good (the Law) and turned it into both a burden on the people and an idol that the Pharisees had grown to worship. The Law was no longer the means to experience a full relationship with God—it *was* their god.

The Pharisees are not alone in their desire to know what rules and regulations they need to obey in order to draw closer to God. We all want that—it's human nature that makes grace so difficult to accept. When it comes to investing, Faith Driven Investors have often been no different. We've built hedges around what we can and cannot do and instead of actively engaging in good work, we've focused on avoiding that which we perceive as negative or sinful.

As a group, we've become known for what we are *against* rather than what we are *for*. Does this mean that we should embrace all things? No. But it does mean we can miss the opportunity to be known primarily for what we're *for* in the world, as opposed to what we stand against.

WHAT WE ARE AGAINST

Faith Driven Investors have differing opinions on which industries should be avoided, but their lists often include some combination of abortifacients, adult entertainment, gambling, tobacco, alcohol, firearms, manufacturing and mining technologies that harm the environment, or food sources that are unsustainable. Many investors screen assets that touch these markets out of their portfolios in an effort to effect corporate policy change through discourse.

In many cases, screening is a healthy practice. There are certain things that Christians *should* stand in opposition to, one way or the other. From the aforementioned partial list of problematic areas, adult entertainment and abortifacients are two issues believers will largely agree on. However, the methodologies for *how* we act differently as Faith Driven Investors are varied, even on these two issues.

This is particularly true as we move down the list of industries that are problematic. We are called to respond to God's Word and the presence of the Holy Spirit in our lives, but *how* we are called to respond is hardly a one-size-fits-all answer. Among the long list of problematic markets, we can find ourselves on a slippery slope where the difference between our opinions, beliefs, and convictions gets muddy. God's truth isn't muddy, but how we take action can be. You can easily talk to two separate Faith Driven Investors and get different answers about which screens are and are not effective. Does that mean one is right and one is wrong? Not necessarily.

Opinions are transient, formed regularly, and evolve quickly as data emerges. Beliefs have more staying power but can shift based on data and lived experiences. Convictions are powerful, lifelong truths that we should be prepared to debate vigorously while defending them. Collectively, they create a lens through which other information passes. An ideal balance of these three terms is to have a multitude of opinions, plenty of beliefs, and a handful of convictions. For Faith Driven Investors, most of our convictions should be derived from our Christian faith, which is inextricably linked to an understanding of what it means to love God and love our neighbor—the two greatest commandments that Jesus lays out for us. As we collectively and individually go through this discernment process, we must have an abundance of grace with each other, even as we sharpen one another's thinking in love.

When we treat our opinions as if they're convictions, we run the risk of doing ourselves a disservice. The early Faith Driven Investing movement was largely about what we screened out of our portfolios. This wasn't a bad thing. For me and my family, and for many other believers I know, it's an important part of our strategy. Yet what we avoid has come to define too much of our legacy as Christian investors. The Bible promises more than that.

Part of the problem is that it's easier to avoid things than it is to engage with them. That's also true in life, not just investing. It's easier to ignore a homeless person than it is to ask them how you can help. It's easier to keep conversations with neighbors at a surface level than it is to try to understand how they're really doing, what they really believe, and why.

God didn't call us to comfort—he didn't invite us to take the easy way out. There's a reason the path is narrow. When we focus *only* on negative screening, we're capturing an incomplete picture. We run the risk of doing what the Pharisees did with the law. It can become a game of one-upmanship where we see who can draw the lines tighter and tighter. Consequently, Faith Driven Investing starts to be about cultural avoidance and cultural withdrawal rather than cultural engagement. I think that's the best case to be made for positive screening.

We are called to lean in, with truth shared in love, and celebrate great things that God is doing in and through the marketplace. We must seek out, embrace, and pour ourselves into the creation of new things. We must find businesses and organizations that are rooting out sin in the world, directly or indirectly. We must think about restoration, in anticipation of a "new heaven and a new earth" coming to be (Revelation

21:1). We must do the work to find businesses that are actually standing *for* things.

Bible scholar N. T. Wright does a great job describing the "Four-Part Gospel"—Creation, Fall, Redemption, and Restoration.[1] I grew up with the middle two, but Wright unpacks all four narratives. Of these four, three are positive (Creation, Redemption, and Restoration) and only *one* is negative. So when we think about what we are *for*, we want to be able to tie into three of these four parts. Creation, redemption, and restoration involve moving *toward* something. The Fall describes something to avoid. It's a simple metric, but I'm a simple guy!

Looking at these four parts, 75 percent of them suggest how we invest through positive screens as opposed to avoidance. That's just one way to look at our strategy and to try to find a balance between negative screens, positive screens, and active engagement. We want to find companies we can embrace while also acknowledging that some avoidance is appropriate.

In our work at Sovereign's Capital, we largely think about what we want to embrace. What do we want to engage in? How can we identify entrepreneurs and business leaders who are *creating* new things, *redeeming* broken things, and *restoring* the world to God's original design?

With these guides, there is plenty of room for individual interpretation and the leading of the Holy Spirit. At

Sovereign's Capital, this framework has helped our thinking materially. Instead of being solely focused on the type
of investments we avoid, we get to focus on the leaders and
business models that we want to support and encourage—
concepts and ideas that promote human flourishing, creation care, and narratives that reflect God's plan for humanity.
Here's how this works in real life.

WHAT GRAB IS FOR

Anthony Tan had the idea for Grab about the same time that
Uber was being born in the United States. What he realized,
and what I saw firsthand as I was living in Southeast Asia
with my family at the time, was that safe and accessible public transportation there was nonexistent. Japan and Europe
have incredible train systems, but nothing like this existed
in Southeast Asia. Taxis and private car services were the primary options.

Anthony realized that there were millions of riders getting
in taxis every day all over his home country of Malaysia who
were uncertain about the common things you'd expect from
a taxi service. *What am I going to get charged for when I try to
get out of this taxi? How long is it going to take me to get there?
Am I going to be cheated? Am I going to get dropped off in a bad
part of town and mugged?* All these issues for riders made it
unsafe, and much of that insecurity was hurting women and
children the most.

But the problem didn't stop with the riders. Taxi drivers faced uncertainty around earned wages, knowing their taxi company would take a huge cut out of what they made. They were left wondering if they were going to get paid at the end of the week and if they'd be able to put food on the table for their families. In light of that ambiguity, drivers often ended up taking matters into their own hands and extorted the riders who got into their taxis, just to make sure they'd get paid.

All of that made for a messy, broken system, and Anthony stepped squarely into the middle of it. He created a company that stands for safety, transparency, and reliability. Now, Grab is the largest technology startup in Southeast Asian history, has acquired Uber in the region, and went on to populate every country in Southeast Asia with over five million drivers on their platform, as well as two million merchants that rely on Grab financial services (a parallel business unit to transportation).

What makes Anthony's story powerful is that he didn't set out to attack the broken system. He wasn't trying to tear down the taxi companies. In fact, while Uber disintermediated taxi companies, Anthony worked *with* the existing players to equip them with services that would make the whole ecosystem better. His goal was to create something that stood for certain values, knowing that defining his company by what it was for would be better than marking it only by what it was against.

THE MISSION OF 410 MEDICAL

Another example in a completely different field is 410 Medical, whose "mission is to help save the lives of critically ill patients by developing innovative tools that assist health care providers in improving resuscitation."[2] The name comes from two things. One, 40 ml/kg in 10 minutes is the calculation of fluid delivery goals in pediatric septic shock. 410 Medical has sought to help providers meet this goal in every patient. Two, the founders were inspired by 1 Peter 4:10, which says, "Each of you should use whatever gift you have received to serve others, as faithful stewards of God's grace in its various forms."

That's exactly what they're doing. Mark Piehl is the chief medical officer and cofounder of 410 Medical. He's also a pediatric intensive care physician at WakeMed Children's Hospital in Raleigh, North Carolina, where he takes care of the sickest of the sick kids every day. His work drives what 410 Medical is for. And what 410 Medical is *for* is life-saving capabilities in the hands of health care providers treating pediatric patients, adults, and soldiers with rapid delivery of fluids. One of the leading causes of death is shock—septic shock, hemorrhagic shock, and other forms of shock that actually show up millions of times every year. So 410 is equipping doctors and nurses to be able to deliver lifesaving fluid in a patient's most critical hour of need.

To date, this technology has saved thousands and thousands of lives. These are not patients who come in and simply get hooked up to an IV drip. These are patients who come in after enduring terrible situations and are on the verge of dying. How do you get three or four liters of fluid into a patient whose whole system has collapsed because they don't have any blood pressure? You have to have a way to precisely deliver large amounts of fluid into a patient in a timely manner.

Mark and his team created a way to do this, and now they work with five of the top ten children's hospitals in the world. They have received multiple grants from the US military to develop a more rugged version to go with deployed field-based medics to the battlefield. But again, this is a company that isn't about trying to fix something that's broken in the health care system (though there's plenty worth fixing). They are operating out of a creative mandate that has afforded them the ability to come up with a unique solution to a common problem. They're now taking that solution and trying to make it available to as many patients and health care providers as possible. Most of these patients don't return home with permanent wounds; they recover to total functionality.

HOW SLTC PROVIDES MEANINGFUL WORK

Another company we love is SLTC—Southeast Lineman Training Center. They bring in high school graduates and people coming out of the military and give them access to meaningful work. These are predominantly young men, but also a few young women, who have decided that they want to work with their hands. They want to work outdoors. They want to travel. They don't want to sit at a desk in an office. They want stable and honorable work. And they don't want to incur debt to have access to this work. They want to be able to provide a great income for their families.

The maintenance and construction of new electrical grids is a critically important component of our national infrastructure. SLTC is the premier trade school for high voltage electrical linemen in the country. On the one hand, it's a dirty job, right? They climb telephone poles, hook up what needs to be hooked up, and then drive down the road to the next destination. When the wildfires happened in California, they had to deal with all the downed power lines. It's the same drill in New Orleans when a hurricane blows through. And yet these are skilled tradespeople who run *toward* the storm. In our greatest hour of need as communities, these are the brave folks who get the lights, heat, internet, and phones turned back on.

SLTC has created a culture where these young men and women understand that they're a part of something. They are imbued with the meaning that their job has. They are providing valuable services to people, and they know it. The SLTC team is focused on reminding their trainees that they're maintaining a nation's way of life and building a better way of life for the many people around the world who don't have steady access to power.

The program is simple and runs for fifteen weeks. At the end, the placement rate for graduates is 95 percent, and the average starting salary is more than $70,000. For those willing to work a bit of overtime and travel, making north of six figures (without having incurred debt) is a very real possibility.

The number of Americans in their twenties with no debt is a vast minority, but SLTC is adding more to their number with each graduating class. They're taking people who don't have college degrees and giving them an opportunity to do honorable work that provides for their families. And, as SLTC trains these talented men and women, they are pouring into all aspects of their growth and development—financial planning, character, and spiritual formation.

SLTC's legacy is that they are both helping to create and maintain the infrastructure of our nation and equipping individuals to have meaningful work for a lifetime. They are loving these graduates well both during and after their educational journey.

BEING FOR SOMETHING REQUIRES RISK

At the end of the day, it's easy to define ourselves by what we are against. That's not risky. But if we're trying to invest and eliminate any and all risk, then we're never going to put a dollar toward anything. We have to acknowledge that systems are broken, people are broken, and we're going to

make mistakes. We're never going to be able to fully eliminate sin from our portfolios. We just can't. As long as we
invest in people on this side of heaven, we are investing in
sinners.

And yet, it's our job to lean in and be cultural change
agents rather than retreating into a holy huddle. There will
always be messiness. There are still companies in our portfolio that aren't living up to their missional potential. They
are not completely seizing the opportunity that God has put
in front of them. Do their imperfections mean we should
divest? Of course not. Instead, we lean in and ask questions.
How can we change this? How do we do a better job filter-
ing? Should we bring in a chaplain or chief spiritual officer?
Those are questions that, had we avoided the company in the
first place, we wouldn't be allowed to ask now.

I don't want to wake up in ten years and have a bunch of
examples where nothing went wrong. I want to have a bunch
of examples where stuff went wrong, but a lot of stuff went
right, too. Ships aren't built to stay in the harbor. They're
designed to go out and sail. But at the same time, they're
also designed with a bilge pump. Why? Because even the
shipbuilder knows that every ship is going to take on water
at some point. As Faith Driven Investors, I believe we are
more like the Marine Corps than the National Guard. We're
called to go out and engage in the conflict instead of man-
ning the defenses.

Faith Driven Investors get to decide what hills we're willing to die on. There are certain negative screens that absolutely should exist. But culture is going to try to bait us into drawing more and more lines in the sand that don't really have to be there. Squabbling about what's permissible and what is not is what the Pharisees spent their whole lives doing.

The reality is that there are just too many cool things being done in the marketplace that we can be radically *for*. That's how I am called to spend the time God has granted to me. At Sovereign's Capital, we are for radically loving our people. We are for radically loving our customers. We are for the provision of an outstanding product or service delivered in a way that celebrates who God made us to be.

Right now, we have to be willing to talk about what's working and not working. It can be tempting to run a fund and keep painting the rosy picture of what we wish were true but really isn't. If Faith Driven Investors want the future to look different, we have to be willing to ruthlessly interrogate ourselves. We have to ask tough questions of each other, most often quietly in a closed setting and not in grandstanding fashion. We must speak truth in love. Have we lost our saltiness? Have we forfeited our opportunity to be light to a world that often feels dark and hostile?

The avoidance strategy has the risk of becoming all salt and no light. Conversely, there's a risk that in being focused on what we're for, we can be all light and no salt. So we have to find the balance and grow comfortable in knowing that we are not perfect but that we're engaging with investments that lean into the world boldly. I say "Onward!" in both truth and love—not for our name's sake, but for Jesus' name's sake.

CHAPTER 6

REFLECTING CREATION BY MAKING NEW THINGS

Cathie Wood

I believe I was born with the gift of faith. The Holy Spirit has been an active presence in my life as my faith has deepened and developed over time. What started as a childlike faith grew into a very real relationship with God. During every different season of my life, God has been the constant.

Being the child of immigrants in the United States, I felt the pressure of carrying the family mantle into college, which brought with it a lot of fear and trepidation. But God stayed with me. When I began my career with Capital Group, my relationship with God only deepened. Then, when I moved to New York to join Jennison Associates as chief economist, analyst, portfolio manager, and managing director, I felt God's presence every step of the way. Even through the various crashes in the stock market, the tech and telecom bust, the 2008–2009 financial meltdown, and my own divorce, I never felt like God was leaving me or deserting me. He always felt near.

I believe God's standard of success for me in both the financial world and in my life is to simply follow his will. This compass is what has guided me throughout the course of my life, starting with some stocks that no one else wanted.

SERENDIPITOUS STOCKS

When I started at Jennison, I was beginning to think about the markets in a different way. I was in economics, but I really wanted to get into equity research. So Sig Segalas, the chief investment officer, told me I could move over, but he said I'd have to find my own universe. Basically, he reminded me that because the analysts were lifers, they weren't going to give me any of their stocks.

Because I couldn't analyze what the others at the firm were, I had to wait for new ideas to come along, particularly ideas that seemed to fall through the cracks because nobody wanted them. I felt like a little dog under the table scrapping for crumbs.

This situation ended up being serendipitous for me because, at the time, something called database publishing evolved. The technology analyst didn't want it because it had publishing in the name, and the publishing analyst didn't want it because it had technology in the name, so it fell to me. Suddenly, Reuters and Telerate were my stocks, and of course, because of their technology and content strategies, they ended up being precursors to the internet.

The same thing happened again with wireless. No one wanted Vodafone. First of all, it was a foreign stock at the time, and no one thought these big brick phones were ever going to amount to anything. Then the opposite happened, and we all know how the wireless industry ended up. While I say that I got my start picking up the stocks that others ignored, really I was participating in the earliest manifestation of the convergence between and among technologies, which I believe is moving into overdrive right now and creating amazing investment opportunities.

The ideas that others dismissed or discarded became the ones I wanted and the ones I most often ran with. That mentality has never left my approach to investing. Those investments made my career, but they also made me appreciate innovation. I was able to experience the power of innovation, how much it's underestimated in the early days, and how exponentially explosive growth can be over time.

For us, and for many, everything changed in the 2008–2009 financial meltdown. That period of time for our strategy at AllianceBernstein led to our pulling a lot of the risk out of our portfolios. I became more unsettled because the firm became more quantitatively driven and compared everyone's short-term performance to broad-based benchmarks. We were supposed to take our cues from companies that had experienced success in the past, which was not consistent with our philosophy.

I couldn't have been more opposed to this idea. That approach is anathema to productive investing. What I care about is disruptive innovation, which is another way of saying "creative destruction." I wanted (and still want today) to research the "Big Ideas" that will transform the way the world works. The opposite of that is what you see when the S&P 500 and the NASDAQ populate their benchmarks increasingly with "value traps" created by stocks that are cheap for a reason.

I believe benchmarks are where the big risks are long-term because they fill up with companies that have done very well historically but are going to be disintermediated and disrupted by the massive amount of innovation that's taking place. Meta, formerly Facebook, is a good example. TikTok came from nowhere! Today, passive and benchmark-sensitive investing is contributing to the most massive misallocation of capital in history. Consider also that Jesus once told a parable that mentioned the "deceitfulness of wealth" (Mark 4:19). I believe that investing in companies because of their past success can be a trap.

Still, everyone around me continued to embrace this concept in a big way, meaning I became more and more of an odd duck within my own firm. It got to the point where, because the strategy I managed was "too volatile," I was told to risk-control it with benchmarks. That was the writing on the wall for me. What happened next is what I still do today.

BUILDING ARK

I started ARK Invest at the age of fifty-seven, so it was quite late in my career. I did a lot of soul-searching, for both personal and professional reasons, leading up to the decision to go out on my own. Part of that meant going to the Bible and saying, "Okay God, tell me what you want me to do." It seemed like over and over again, I kept coming back to passages about the Ark of the Covenant. What I learned is that the Israelites would take the Ark into battle with them, and with the Ark came the presence of God.

I realized that I needed the presence of God to lead me, protect me, defend me, poke me, prod me, and be part of my decision. I wouldn't have founded the company if it hadn't been for God doing just that.

I came into a house of complete silence, which was something that never happened, but the children were all out at activities, so I had some time alone. I remember walking over to the kitchen island and feeling shocked that it was so quiet. I said to myself, *Wow, this has never happened to me before.*

As soon as that thought crossed my mind, I felt a *wham!* in my chest, which I truly believe was the Holy Spirit hitting me with inspiration, saying, *Okay, this is the plan.* And the idea that came to mind was that I'd basically been a student of disruptive innovation my entire career. What was stopping me from disrupting my own industry? I knew what was broken. I knew how new technologies could help. I knew social media and other people, even competitors, could come in and make everything in our industry different and better. So I did, and that's where ARK Invest came from.

At the time, most people thought that a fully active, transparent equity ETF wouldn't work. They didn't think my style of investing made sense, but that's because it was completely different from what people knew. I had to blaze a trail not only in the way ARK invested but also in the way we researched.

Instead of having analysts follow industries and sectors, we had them follow technologies. We wanted analysts who were specialists in technologies and generalists in industries. But then we did what people really couldn't understand—we started giving away our research. Our thought process was simple: we want to engage with and become a part of the communities we're researching. We wanted to transform our own industry with the technologies that we were watching transform other industries, and we believed this required a communal effort.

For the first three years, I funded ARK all by myself. And for those first three years, our assets didn't grow much at all. I really thought that if I built it, people would come. I had a wide network and lots of clients, but what I didn't understand was that the ETF world and the traditional investment world I had come from did not communicate. They didn't understand each other at all.

I had fallen into the trap that many entrepreneurs fall into: not understanding the market completely. We sat basically still for three years until we landed a large institutional mandate in March 2016 and then a distribution deal in July 2016. But until 2016, we were more or less stuck at $30–40 million and losing a lot of money.

Now, did I think we were going to fail? No, I really didn't. I know that others saw our needle not moving and doubted us. There's something called the deathwatch for ETFs, and we may have made it onto that deathwatch list at one point, but I never thought we were going to fail. While I was pouring a significant amount of my wealth into the company, I just kept praying. I knew God was with me. Even if we failed, I knew that this leap of faith had been the right thing to do. It was about God's will, not my own.

CREATING WITH THE CREATOR

I mentioned earlier that one of the initial problems that pushed me to start ARK was benchmarking, the idea of looking at past success as a barometer for future success. Instead, I wanted to invest in the companies that were creating something new where nothing like it had existed before—the disruptors. Part of the Israelites' story is that after God rescued them from Egypt, they had to create the Ark of the Covenant and the Tabernacle—the objects that marked God's presence with them—from scratch. When you're working with the materials and plans God has given you, you can't look at what other nations have done or adopt ideas that may have worked in the past. Instead, as we see in Exodus 35, God gave the Israelites (specifically two men, Bezalel and Oholiab) exactly what they needed:

> He has filled them with skill to do all kinds of work
> as engravers, designers, embroiderers in blue, purple
> and scarlet yarn and fine linen, and weavers—all of
> them skilled workers and designers.
>
> EXODUS 35:35

These gifts come with a responsibility to use them well. We see the same in Jesus' Parable of the Talents in the New Testament. When God gives you something, there's an expectation that you do good with it. Furthermore, there's an invitation to participate in what he's doing here on earth.

God gives us the chance to work alongside him, to be his coworkers. He wants us to join him in starting, sharing, completing, and investing in new projects, ideas, and businesses. This has been true since the Garden of Eden, when God tasked Adam with tending the plants and naming the animals. There's the possibility of a shared vision between God and his people. This is the creation mandate. This is what God has called us to do.

That's why God wants to use us to bring about his Kingdom on earth as it is in heaven. Our creations (our businesses, our investments) can bring order out of chaos, solve problems, utilize innovation, provide solutions—all to create a better world.

This truth should empower us. It should give us the ability to invest in innovative ideas with confidence, knowing that those are the very things God is likely to use to move his work forward. That's what Faith Driven Investors should strive to do every day.

With ARK, I feel like we've been given an idea to invest in a way that builds businesses that grow, change, and improve the world radically. I believe we have been put here on earth not to mimic what might have happened historically but to create and innovate and transform the world into a better place to live. When I see the success of Tesla and the other technology stocks we've taken risks to invest in, I sense God giving me a greater responsibility to do more good work with what comes back with the investment returns.

That's why I continue to look ahead, to invest in what's new and what's next. We're seeing growth happen through innovations in DNA sequencing that are going to trans-form health care. For the first time, we have the technology that can identify among the six billion bits of code in our genome where there are mutations or programming errors. Along with artificial intelligence and gene therapies, genomic sequencing is going to help us cure diseases.

Then, there's the new technology in robotics. While many people worry about robots taking away jobs, we're working to show that while they may take over mundane tasks, this adds to the productivity gains of countries around the world and therefore adds to wage gains because the jobs being created are a much higher value add.

For those who are really concerned about the environment, electric vehicles, and particularly their battery technology, are only getting better. We're going to transform the world from the internal combustion engine to battery technology. And as costs continue to fall, we're expecting to see electric vehicles on a massive scale.

Artificial intelligence is another example where we're seeing costs fall fast enough to accelerate the rate at which people can adopt the technology. When we're talking about artificial intelligence, we're talking about the ability to make better, more well-informed decisions faster. According to our research, artificial intelligence training costs are dropping at a rate of more than 60 percent per year.[1] Think about what happens when the cost of something drops that rapidly. That means more and more researchers and businesspeople will harness it to make their businesses better and their lives better.

And then finally, there's blockchain technology. According to ARK's research, Bitcoin represents the first global monetary system, a private (non-government), digital, rules-based monetary system that my mentor, Art Laffer, thinks is wonderful. Then there's decentralized finance (DeFi), which is built on top of Ethereum. DeFi is going to take away a lot of the intermediary roles in financial services and thereby take away the friction, increase yields, and lower lending rates. Lastly, NFTs (non-fungible tokens) are the first global, digital, private (non-government), immutable property rights system. As economists Hernando de Soto and Thomas Sowell have taught us, giving people property rights is the best and quickest way to pull them and their countries out of poverty.

These are just some of the tools we've been given to create a better world. For me, it's about allocating capital to serve God's creation in the most innovative and creative ways possible. This is part of the process through which things can be made new. It's an invitation from God to create alongside him, and it's a call that we all can accept today.

CHAPTER 7

REDEFINING RETURN

Greg Lernihan

My Faith Driven Investing journey began in 2012 after my first trip to Haiti. I returned home a changed man, questioning the priorities of my life. A few months later, my family decided to sell the majority interest in our company to a private equity firm. There comes a time in life when many faith-driven people ask themselves, *Am I doing what God has called me to do?* At the time, I was the cofounder of a fast-growing technology company. Despite loving my job and leading our company, I felt the gentle nudge of the Holy Spirit inviting me to do something different and to pursue a life of purpose and significance.

I originally thought this life was going to be in the nonprofit world. I quickly learned that Americans have been consistently giving only about 2 percent of GDP for the last forty years (in 2019, donations were $450 billion). It's called the stubborn giving curve. I also learned that there are 1.5 million nonprofits in the United States, all seeking financial support from a relatively small pool of funds that isn't growing!

PHILANTHROPIC VS. INVESTMENT CAPITAL

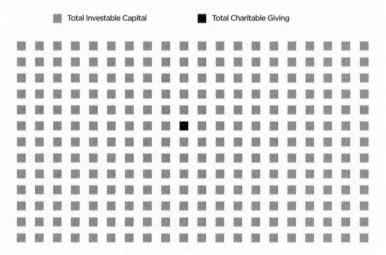

I learned that the United Nations estimates that globally we will need two to three trillion dollars per year to solve some of our major social issues like hunger, poverty, education, and health care. It also became clear that while philanthropic capital is important, it can't begin to solve our growing social problems. It was obvious that to solve these problems, we need access to private capital, a pool of funds that currently is in excess of $100 trillion and growing. Money is available. We now need to find great for-profit entrepreneurs to help solve some of our social challenges. We need both investable and charitable capital to begin to attack our problems.

When we started our family fund back in 2013, we had only a philanthropic focus. Within months, we also created a family fund that we reserved for impact investments. At that time, we entered the space from a secular perspective. We weren't familiar with or connected to Faith Driven Investing back then, but we started reaching out to other Christians and connecting with like-minded investors and thought leaders. We attended several events, including The Gathering and Praxis's annual conference.

Through networking, we quickly connected with Christian leaders in the faith-driven space. This created a lightbulb moment for us. We immediately switched our investment criteria and began investing from a triple bottom line perspective, seeking spiritual, social, and financial returns. Until that point in time, we were focused only on social and financial returns.

This was an "aha" moment for us. We were shocked to learn that we could invest in Christian entrepreneurs who led companies with a spiritual lens, were committed to making a social impact, and delivered a financial return.

After years of prayer about how to use the capital and talent that God had bestowed on us, we finally realized these aren't our resources—they're God's. This was a life-changing moment for our family. I have been a Christian my entire life, but this was a new perspective. We had always tithed, but we never worried about managing our other resources for the Lord.

My wife asked me to write in my prayer journal asking the Lord to help us manage our resources. I wrote the following: "Lord, help me to get comfortable with giving all of our assets away. Help me see that these resources are not ours. Give me the wisdom and courage to steward them as you would want me to." I distinctly remember not wanting to write this in my prayer journal, as I really didn't want it to come true. Thankfully, I married a godly woman who encouraged and challenged our family to think from a Kingdom perspective.

It finally became clear that we are stewarding God's capital and that none of it belongs to us. This changed our view significantly and started us thinking about how we would invest *his* capital. We now get up every morning trying to steward God's resources rather than trying to invest ours. When you allow God to be your financial advisor, everything changes.

FOUR-QUADRANT INVESTING

Our family investment discussions are usually about how we can steward God's resources, while also taking appropriate risks. We don't want to bury the talents God has given us.

Because everything we have is God's, taking risks isn't the key concern—it's trusting him. That's the journey of any Faith Driven Investor. It might be the hardest part because when you're evaluating investments, you really don't know which investments are going to be financially successful, and you don't want to waste God's resources. When you put a faith lens on your investments, it gets even harder.

After a couple of years of investing, we decided to graph all our investments on a 2x2 grid. On the X-axis was financial returns, and on the Y-axis was social and spiritual returns.

STEWARDING HIS RESOURCES

SPIRIT-LED	MAXIMIZING TALENTS
BURIED TALENTS	CAPITALISTIC

Social & Spiritual Return →

Financial Return →

The lower left quadrant had low social, spiritual, and financial returns, which is where no one wants to be—it's the mistake quadrant. In our case, we called this quadrant "buried talents" to be consistent with the Parable of the Talents.

In the lower right box, we had investments that were getting high financial returns, but low or no spiritual or social returns. We called this quadrant "capitalistic." Nearly all the invested capital in the world is in this quadrant. These investments are seeking the highest returns first and foremost.

The so-called "winning quadrant" in a classic 2x2 is always in the upper right corner. These investments return high social, spiritual, and financial returns. Every Faith Driven Investor wants their investments to be in this quadrant. We call it the "maximizing talents" quadrant.

When we graphed all of our investments, we noticed that we had investments in the upper left quadrant as well. These investments would produce high social and high spiritual returns but low financial returns. At first, we weren't sure how to understand this. These investments didn't seem strategic on our part, and we weren't sure whether this quadrant represented true investment excellence, even for a Faith Driven Investor. We originally thought that all our investments should be in the "maximizing talents" quadrant. Again, the winning box is always the upper right quadrant! Yet our portfolio had a number of investments in the upper left quadrant.

We looked at the companies in this quadrant and noticed that many of these investments were ones we would reference to other investors when we were asked for examples of impact investments. They were some of our favorite entrepreneurs and companies.

It was immediately clear that we couldn't financially justify why we made the investments in this upper left quadrant.

By design, as you slide further to the upper right in the 2x2, there is always an investment with a higher return. But nearly every investment in the upper left quadrant moved us.

We decided that if all the business opportunities we invest in looked perfect on paper, then where were we allowing God to show his majesty and his power so we can give him glory in impossible situations? We realized that the upper left quadrant investments require the Holy Spirit's intervention to be successful.

About half of our investments in the upper left quadrant are debt versus equity. In some cases we use charitable capital, and in others we use personal capital. Investing in this quadrant doesn't mean we are bad investors. However, it does mean that we are accepting a lower financial return for a purpose we believe in.

We aren't going into these investments to lose money, but we believe strongly in the entrepreneur, the company's mission, or the impact they can have—so much so that we are okay with any outcome.

Because these are God's resources and not ours, we need to evaluate investments from his perspective. This means reorienting ourselves to define what makes an excellent investment. We're looking at more than just numbers on a spreadsheet. We're attempting to invest from a faith-driven perspective and asking God for advice on how he'd like to see his resources deployed.

Aimee Minnich, cofounder of Impact Foundation, says that an "excellent investment" is one where the overlapping circles of expectations and reality are as close as possible. When we invest through this four-quadrant method, we're trying to outline clearer expectations that hopefully match the realistic outcome. That requires that we look at more than just financial returns. We must define all of our expectations.

After much debate, we ended up calling the upper left quadrant the "Spirit-led" quadrant. It became clear to us that we wouldn't be investing in this quadrant unless we were led by the Holy Spirit. This quadrant requires a different investment philosophy. Praxis describes it as "I sacrifice, we win," a redemptive philosophy.

What's different about investing in this quadrant? We learned there are four things:

- It's biblical,
- We are employing the marginalized,
- These companies have great difficulty raising capital, and
- The Spirit-led entrepreneurs themselves are faith-filled leaders who inspire us!

Biblical

Our faith in God and our faith in the entrepreneur supersedes our fear of losing money or receiving lower returns. We know from the Bible that Jesus invites us to meet him where he is. And time after time in Scripture, he is with the weak, the destitute, and the lonely. Oftentimes investments in the Spirit-led quadrant involve businesses that work with those who most would overlook. Our family's concern is that if we don't meet Jesus where he is, we may miss him entirely.

Employing the Marginalized

This is the quadrant where we are employing the marginalized—people who lack employable skills. They're formally incarcerated returning citizens or unskilled people. In developing countries, they're from hard-to-reach rural areas, or they're farmers and artisans in places where they don't have job opportunities. They're the uneducated or undereducated, and many are women who are taking care of their families. It is valuable to invest money to support these people even if we don't see a significant financial return on our investment.

Difficulty in Raising Capital

The third difference in the Spirit-led quadrant is the difficulty that these entrepreneurs have in raising capital. These companies generally don't have exits with a strategic buyer or with private equity. Most of our investments in this quadrant are loans. With a Spirit-led investment, we have different goals. Scaling isn't the leading objective—survivability and sustainability are.

Spirit-Led Entrepreneurs

The last major difference is the Spirit-led entrepreneurs themselves. They care more about impacting humanity than they do about earning higher financial returns. Most of the investments we have in the "Spirit-led" quadrant are with women and people of color. This is very motivating to us.

In our experience, "Spirit-led" founders are incredibly humble leaders. They care about serving the poor, helping the marginalized, and doing God's work through the business, and that is their focus. Just being around them makes us better people. They are the hands and feet of Christ.

INVESTMENTS FROM THE HEART

To invest in the "Spirit-led" quadrant, you must resist the current that is pulling you to the upper right quadrant ("maximizing talents") that promises better returns. Inherently, being in the "Spirit-led" quadrant means there is always a better financial return available somewhere else—always.

At the end of the day, our investment philosophy is less about finding the best return and more about stewarding God's resources appropriately. We desire to invest in enterprises with the intention to generate measurable, beneficial, social, environmental, spiritual, and financial returns. This is impact investing.

Two keywords that define impact investing are *intentional* and *measurable*. You need to have a plan and purpose that you're driving to achieve so that your investment strategy can clearly support your mission. For example, one investor may be very focused on providing jobs in an impoverished area. If that area is geographically specific, we can measure our success. Is the unemployment rate going down? Are the average wages going up? Are their children now going to school? Do they have medical benefits? These are measurable social issues that faith-driven investments can address.

You can also look at the person leading the company in which you're investing. Are they a faithful Christian? Do their colleagues have good things to say about them? Is their leadership style honorable and respectable? Do they use biblical principles to run their company? Is the leadership willing to share their faith openly throughout the company? These are hard questions to ask, but when they're answered and are part of the company's strategy, they are more attractive to Faith Driven Investors.

In the Spirit-led quadrant, we care more about spiritual and social impact than we do financial returns. There are more factors involved in our decision than just financial statements. We want to see money move companies, businesses, and societies toward human flourishing as outlined in the Bible. Some of these investments will provide a good financial return while also achieving their business objectives, but we also recognize that some won't. However, each quadrant comes with its own respective upside.

For most people, starting in that upper right quadrant and investing in funds makes the most sense. Please understand that any time you consider investing in the "Spirit-led" quadrant, it's very, very difficult. As investors, we have been taught our entire lives to seek high returns in as short a time as possible with the least amount of risk possible. When you're in the "Spirit-led" investment quadrant, it's always higher risk, generally lower returns, and sometimes longer investment periods. It's not about making as much as you can as quickly as you can. It's about a patient and intentional approach to investing that seeks spiritual, social, and financial returns.

There's over $1 trillion currently in donor-advised funds and foundations. Using charitable capital to invest in faith-driven companies is a wonderful idea. Working with groups like the National Christian Foundation and Impact Foundation can help you make this happen. People use donor-advised funds like a charitable checking account. They can make an initial contribution into the donor-advised fund account (which immediately qualifies for an income tax deduction) and then recommend grants from the fund to charities. Donor-advised funds also allow people to choose how they'd like the money in their fund to be invested over time. Impact Foundation helps people ask and answer this question: Where is your passion encouraging you to strategically allocate the money God has entrusted to you? We should be asking this question with both our giving and our investing dollars.

We certainly don't have all the answers. We know that God equips and challenges everyone differently, and we respect that. Today, our family invests by looking through a faith lens. We also serve a different financial advisor and have other measurements besides financial. We don't believe that Jesus would only invest in the "maximizing talents" quadrant (upper right) and focus on 20-percent-plus returns. We believe that Faith Driven Investing spans across both the "Spirit-led" and the "maximizing talents" quadrants.

Initially, we worried that we were sacrificing too much by investing in the "Spirit-led" quadrant, but these investments no longer feel sacrificial to our family. We believe it's the right way to steward God's resources that he has entrusted to us.

We've set a goal that 50 percent of our investments will be in the "Spirit-led" quadrant and 50 percent in the "maximizing talents" quadrant. This isn't intended to be prescriptive, but it's the balance we've found works best for us.

We all know that grants alone won't solve our social issues going forward. They serve an important purpose, and it's critical that all of us continue to grant money to worthy ministries. But investment capital must be an additional part of the equation if we hope to solve global social issues.

As Faith Driven Investors and Christians, we hope to be a part of the solution. Philanthropic capital was a good start, but we now have other options, including personal and charitable capital. It's time to take the next step. Because as Christians, if we don't invest in Spirit-led investments, who will?

PART 2

THEREFORE, THEY...

CHAPTER 8

FIND BEAUTY IN BROKEN THINGS

John and Ashely Marsh

John

Within just a year or two of having our son, Ash and I were three days away from a divorce. We were fighting for custody of Nelson, I was a drug addict, and we were $1.5 million in debt and $99,000 overdrawn. Our lives were upside down. Everything was broken.

Ashely

I didn't know that John was a drug addict when we got married. I was broken in my own ways from different experiences in my own life, and I don't think either one of us fully realized what we were bringing the other person into. When you mix two broken people together like that with all the unaddressed baggage, a tremendous amount of hurt and strife is waiting.

At the time when we were nearing a divorce, John was working twenty hours a day. We were extremely in debt. We didn't have a relationship at all. And I sought a relationship with someone else that turned into a physical and adulterous relationship. Three years into our marriage, we were going through a divorce and fighting for the custody of our oldest child, Nelson.

John

The pressure built, and I kept hearing a voice in the back of my head telling me that my life was not worth living and I should take my own life. I went up to the attic of our old, historic house where the junk scattered around seemed like a picture of the life we had made for ourselves. Broken things were everywhere. I moved an old fan out of the way and set up a rope. That's where I was going to hang myself.

But then the voice in my head changed. Instead of hearing someone whispering, *Kill yourself*, which I had been hearing for months, I heard a different phrase: *Die to yourself*. Instead of *Take your life*, it was *Lay your life down*. They sounded so similar to me, but I knew something needed to change. So instead of taking my life, I cried out to a God I had never known and was absolutely transformed. It was like lightning had struck me, and every hair on my body stood up. Suddenly, love got past the fence I had built, and for the first time in my life I didn't feel the pain, the suffering, or the regret I had been carrying. I felt free. I was totally loved.

I came out of that place on fire for the work I was going to do and addicted to God's love. I walked downstairs and told Ash what I had just experienced and what I thought was the voice of God speaking to me. I told her that God had touched me and transformed me, that love had gotten past the fence. I told her that God had poured his love out on me and transformed me in that place.

Ashely

John told me that he didn't want to get a divorce anymore because he was following God now. I looked straight at him and said, "You're a liar. You've always been a liar. You're not going to follow God." There had been so many times earlier in our marriage when he had promised to change and hadn't. He had sworn to be different, and he had failed to follow through over and over again. He may have wanted to change, but he was hopeless to do so.

Not long after John's experience in the attic, I found out I was pregnant. I didn't know if it was John's child or the child of the man I was having an adulterous relationship with, but after twelve weeks, I had a miscarriage. John and I were completely broken down. Things just flat out couldn't get any worse. I was mad. I was mad at myself, mad at God, and mad at anybody I crossed paths with.

But then God met me personally like he had met John, and we were both saved.

John

Ash met God in the middle of our dirty living room floor. That's just how God came into our story. Wherever there was a mess, wherever there was dirt, he showed up. From then on, we gave up trying to do things alone. We prayed. And we surrendered what little we felt we had over to a God we had just barely met.

For seven years, we went to counseling every week and were discipled by an amazing couple who taught us God's Word and showed us that if God had a currency, it would be forgiveness. Slowly we had conversations and made decisions that allowed us to find one another again as we began to build a new life from the redeemed broken pieces of our old life. During this time, we felt like the poster children for broken marriages, yet there was something in our story that gave people a glimpse of hope. We were becoming ambassadors of hope. It wasn't anything we had done, necessarily, but for whatever reason, God had given us a second chance, and through that we were able to help others see that the same opportunity was available to them.

Ashely

We were like a magnet for other broken people because they were attracted to our story and to the hope that it's possible to experience beauty even in the midst of tragedy. That wasn't just what happened to us, but that's what God wanted to do through us.

This story is the foundation that God has built the rest of our life's work on. It's this story that informs how we go about our day-to-day, how we parent, how we lead, and even how we invest and build businesses. Having someone who loved us unconditionally and who crashed into our lives so extravagantly explains not just *how* we do what we do but also *why*.

Everything we're doing today came out of tremendous pain and brokenness. We can say that there's beauty in broken things. We can say that things that are lost and found can be more precious than things that were never lost. We can say that there's hope even in the worst of circumstances. And we can point people to a source of comfort because we, too, have been in need of comfort and have found it in God.

John and Ashely

What does that have to do with investing? Everything.

ALL ABOUT PLACE

We started our construction company with $1,000, going slowly and steadily with small repair jobs on houses in the area, working for one small paycheck at a time. One thing we quickly learned during that season is that God doesn't waste time. All the while, he was working on our respective skill sets. He was using our experiences to prepare us for the work we do today.

God is always taking what you're doing and weaving it into where you're going.

At the same time, we began to put all our resources, our time, our energy, and our dreams into the small town of Opelika, Alabama. The heartbeat of this town is in its name. If you say it quickly and with the right drawl, it sounds like "Hope-ya-like-a." And we think people *do* like it.

This was right where we had our first child, so it felt like the perfect place to start. All our "firsts" happened in these city blocks, so why not build a town we were proud of? We believe that hyperfocus in any area can change it— the closer your contract, the bigger your impact—and that's what happened. We've learned that if we're going to make a place flourish, we need to use the formula Jesus showed us with loaves and fishes. That means we measure, manage, and multiply. And anything we measure and manage faithfully, God will multiply. We don't measure success; we measure faithfulness, because that's what God asks of stewards.

Over time, we've done just that by adding a real estate company to our construction business, and within a few years, we had over one hundred pieces of property we were working to restore. Almost all of these properties were within a ten-block radius. As the real estate company grew, so did the construction business, because at first, we couldn't afford to hire contractors.

From that first business came a historic renovation business, an architectural salvage business, a restaurant group, and now a consulting company, where we help our clients steward projects and portfolios of over $1.5 billion worth of redemptive real estate in nine small towns around the country. All we want to do is help people restore cities through the lens of redemptive real estate that we have learned over the last twenty-five years. We work with towns of 800 people to towns of 180,000-plus people. We do this all with the goal of connecting and creating community. We promote the flourishing of cities with a model that will make your economics teacher and your Sunday school teacher happy.

These are often towns that people might overlook. Our model combines sophisticated real estate development with love. Love is the difference-maker. We coined the term Irreplaceable Real Estates to describe places built by people who don't live anymore, with materials we don't have access to anymore, in methods we don't use anymore, and all of which has been done with love. Because our story is grounded in how God redeemed us—the type of people most might overlook—it's as if these towns were made for us. They come to us with stories of brokenness much like the one we've lived, and out of that we can find hope for the future together.

We are investors, creators, and encouragers of the restoration of amazing places. We believe there is a new asset class being recognized and organized around the irreplaceable downtown real estate that has professional management, aligned and authentic strategy, and thoughtful development. The type of capital and care applied to historic downtowns creates amazing long-term investments and community value that are unmatched. We love that what we invest in hires people and keeps the capital within the community.

Normally, when you do a new building, the process is primarily about the materials and less about labor. When you do a renovation, it's exactly the opposite. It's mostly about the labor and less about the materials, making things a little more complicated. But that's exactly where we think God has called us. In fact, we would suggest that other investments that do not include historic preservation high on the agenda are missing not only a valuable strategy but, like the historic buildings themselves, an irreplaceable one. The forgotten downtown is a new frontier of possibilities.

We believe God cares about places. Throughout Scripture, he is consistently telling people to go to certain places. Jesus' last words to his followers include a list of cities. Place is important to God. The extravagant love we have received brings about a longing and requirement to make a positive difference wherever we find ourselves planted. We know that we can help bring about human flourishing by adding value to people and places that are considered of little or no value because of their brokenness.

So for us, we see broken-down buildings and abandoned cities as places where God wants to be actively involved in the lives of his people. When we look at the town of Opelika, we see a place that has great art, good food, and strong history. But places are like wheelbarrows. Someone has to push them. It takes the consistent stewardship of capital to bring those characteristics to the forefront. We say we have created amazing models to do this, but it's really 80 percent models and 20 percent miracles. That's our plan. Our prayer is to have front-row seats to see God at work.

Isn't that what Faith Driven Investors are called to do—to see the virtues of God, the glimpses of his nature and his personality, in people, places, and things and then do what we can to bring those out? That's what we're doing in Opelika. We're dredging through what many would overlook to help them see that God is there and has been there all along.

COMMUNITY-MINDED CAPITAL

What we realized is that when it comes to saving communities, three types of capital are required: patient capital, properly aligned capital, and productive capital.

For patient capital, we tell investors that they have to be in this for three, five, sometimes seven years. That's the time horizon we operate on. There's often a desire to see immediate returns that are really good, but that's not always our experience. When we first started to go to counseling for our marriage, we had no plans of doing that weekly for seven years. Yet here we are now. The patience required to restore our marriage isn't unlike the patience required to restore a city.

When it comes to properly aligned capital, we believe people need to share the same vision and values. For the vision, they need to want to see the town saved and restored. The values are that they want that work to happen on the right timeline and in the right way. We're talking about creating generational differences here, and so it's important for us to share both a destination and the directions for how we hope to get there.

Lastly, there's productive capital. We think restoring cities should come with a return of your investment and a return on your investment. What we see is that when people rebuild cities out of sheer benevolence, those towns lack sustainability. The change won't last. But we've learned that if we can build things that are sustainable, profitable, and thoughtful, they can have a very long life span.

While we're working with investors who are on a time horizon of a few years, we operate with fifty, seventy-five, or one hundred years into the future on our minds. That's the dream we have for the cities we restore. This is a multigenerational investment. In the same way that the restoration of a marriage ripples down through children and grandchildren, we believe that a town restored, rebuilt, and rejuvenated affects not just the people who live there today but those who come after as well. When sixty people come together, knowing they have the capital to fix what's happening in their city, you have no idea what God can do through that group.

This is the framework we use when we look at investing in places, but we think the same is true for anything a believer puts their money into. We're not only seeking an immediate impact and immediate return. We have an eternal time horizon. Wes Perry, a mentor of ours, taught us to ask, "What could we do for the good of our city that would last fifty years and no one would be able to undo it?" That's our timeline for having an impact in a place.

We also don't invest in businesses that hold up a different set of values from what we've learned from God. And lastly, we don't invest in anything less than excellence because good work done well honors God. These principles are true of Marsh Collective, but they are also true of all Faith Driven Investors. God has saved us from our own brokenness through patience and faithfulness and with eternity in mind. It's our call to go into the world the same way.

The number one priority for us is to meet with God. When we think back to the way we came to know God, strangely, the places we first met with him weren't the places where we were told to be. We didn't meet him in church or in a special moment of a certain song. He met us in our brokenness, in the place where we needed him most. And we believe he offers the same invitation to all people.

There is hope. God loves idiots. Come see us, and if it turns out you think we're so great at building and investing that we could have done this without God, well, don't believe what we're saying. But if you come and see us and you realize we're not all that great, you can know that God is the one doing something great within our work. He is an amazing God who does amazing things. And he's still in the business of taking broken things and turning them into something beautiful. He's done that in our lives, in our towns, and in our businesses, and he offers anyone who would follow him the same thing.

God fixes broken things. So can we.

John

Today, we put love on the income statement and balance sheets, and we've taken business principles and applied them to our marriage. After our boys left the house, Ash came to me and basically said, "Look, I didn't marry you to be away from you. I married you to be with you." So I stepped back as the business leader and Ash stepped forward. She's running all our businesses now, and we're dreaming about growing and building together.

I've quickly learned that if I make a decision without Ash, that's a half-brain decision. She has full veto power. The last time I didn't listen to her—when she shared a feeling from the Holy Spirit and I responded with my own logic—it cost me $7 million. I haven't overrun her since. I know now that feeling ain't nothing and logic ain't everything.

We take the same level of detail we use to steward hundreds of millions of dollars' worth of business with our clients around the country, and we apply that to our marriage. Every week, we have a visionary integrator meeting for our marriage to make sure we're doing what we can to be a high-impact couple. It's more important to me than any other meeting I have. That transformation from being a few days away from divorce to working side by side is supernatural. It could only be done by God.

Ash is my co-visionary. The tools we have learned along the way have given me the amazing opportunity of having the most stimulating conversations with the person I love the most. I didn't even know we could do this. I mean, working with your spouse means you're sleeping with the CFO (or in my case, the CEO) of your company. If you get sideways at work, you're sideways at home. But there's nothing better than working with my wife. It's changed everything.

Ashely

I feel privileged to be a businesswoman in the businesses that John and I have created together and to be doing what we do best, which is helping people and places and changing the hearts of people in towns. John would be the first to tell you that he is great at start-up and expansion but terrible at stabilization. Now, I get to pick up what he has started and carry forward the work we do together. I just love it.

A lot of times, I resented staying in the background as I chose to prioritize being at home and available to the kids. What I've found is that I was using my gifts all along and was just pouting about it because I didn't have any way to frame in my mind that it was valuable.

Now, John and I get to bring in the unique gifts God has equipped us with and use them not only to build businesses but also to build a beautiful marriage and a beautiful life that at one point seemed completely impossible. Now we have the privilege of investing in communities, companies, and other high-impact couples.

What we hope to do through our work and through telling God's story of our lives is to show that there's hope for restoration. There's hope for redemption, not just in businesses and buildings but in people's lives. We care about helping other entrepreneurs, businesses, city-lovers, leaders, and also couples who long to do work together, who want to do life together side by side, and who feel like they can use each other's gifts no matter how diverse they are.

If we can restore people's ability to have open eyes and to hope that God can fix broken things, then I believe that's the greatest gift we can give. We know if there is hope in your future, there is power in your present.

CHAPTER 9

THINK DIFFERENTLY ABOUT RISK

Henry Kaestner

One of the things I love about what I get to do right now is the experience of meeting, talking to, and connecting with other like-minded investors. If people get nothing else from all the work God is doing through Faith Driven Investor and Faith Driven Entrepreneur, I hope they get a taste of the scope and scale through which God's followers are working to bring about his Kingdom on earth as it is in heaven. I get to see this happen every single day, whether we're interviewing podcast guests, exploring deals on Marketplace (the platform we've created to connect Faith Driven Entrepreneurs to Faith Driven Investors), or doing any of the day-to-day work that God has me involved in with these ministries.

Part of that work involves attending and speaking at various conferences where Faith Driven Investors and Faith Driven Entrepreneurs are gathering all around the world. Of course, we host our own annual conferences, but it's always exciting to see what God is doing through other incredible organizations. There is, however, a downside to Christian conferences. And that is the fact that we're all Christians.

Not that being a Christian is a bad thing. Rather, the gathering of people who all believe the same thing can lead to a lack of innovation or interesting ideas. Sometimes when Christians gather, we all nod our heads at the same thing, we comment on subjects about which we all share the same opinions, and we leave never having been challenged at all. This is not true of all Christian conferences, of course, but it can happen.

In the summer of 2021, I attended a conference where someone gave a talk on inflation. After about an hour of hearing fellow Christian investors talk about the different ways to hedge against inflation—whether through precious metals or cryptocurrencies or any of the other ideas along that vein—I realized we were all nodding along to something I was uncertain about.

So I raised my hand and asked the panel of speakers, "Where is the spiritual integration in buying gold bullion?"

No one answered, which I interpreted as encouragement to continue. So I elaborated, wondering aloud why a group of Christian investors should worry about hedging against inflation when we should really be asking ourselves how we should hedge against Judgment Day.

It's my belief, I explained, that the body of Christ simply must come to understand that our investment capital can, and often should, be placed in different investment vehicles and different investment markets where there is a chance for real spiritual growth and Kingdom advancement. If we all believe that we are going to one day give an accounting to God for the way we've spent our lives on earth, it's hard to imagine God is going to ask us what we did to hedge against inflation.

On the other hand, we know for a fact he's going to ask us how we loved and served the people he brought into our lives. He's going to want to know what we did for the least of these. He's going to want to know what we did with the talents he gave us.

After that, there was a lively debate and discussion, but what I took away from that experience has nothing to do with any opinion anyone expressed, my own included. What I learned is that a room full of Christian investors can look a lot like a room full of unbelieving investors. Both groups want to mitigate risk. Both groups want their assets to stay safe and secure. Both groups want to hedge against certain unknowns.

The difference is—or at least should be—that Christian investors have a different understanding of the unknown. Or, to put it another way, Christian investors have a relationship with Someone to whom nothing is unknown. Shouldn't that change the way we invest? Shouldn't that change the way we live?

HEDGES AND PATTERNS

Hedging is a common term in the investing world, but the idea has existed long before there was a stock market. In fact, you may have heard people describe the "hedge around the law" that the Pharisees built in Old Testament times.

For example, as Luke Roush pointed out in chapter 5, while the law required that Israelites not work the twenty-four hours of the Sabbath, some Pharisees would teach that people should not work for twenty-*five* hours, just to be safe. While this mindset may have been well-intentioned, it completely missed the purpose of what God was trying to teach his people. They thought they could retain control. They thought they could do it on their own. But we know that isn't true.

Now, we're seeing that same mindset creep into the hearts of investors. We know what the Bible says about giving, so we obey those verses dutifully, but when it comes to investing, we opt for playing it safe, "just in case." Paul instructs us to "not conform to the pattern of this world, but be transformed by the renewing of [our] mind[s]" (Romans 12:2). Yet the pattern of this world instructs us to have a large retirement account, diversified investments, and even things like a financial nest egg.

Keep in mind, this isn't something I'm observing "out there." This is happening to *me*. If I look at my life, much of what I do regarding my investments amounts to a hedge. Yes, I believe, and I trust in God, but just in case . . . The question I've had to ask myself is, *If I truly believed all that God promises in the Bible, would I act the same way I do, think the same way I do, invest the same way I do?* The concept of hedging in my own life has all too often looked as if it's a hedge against God's promises not being true—just in case he fails to clothe the lilies of the field, just in case he doesn't actually have a plan to prosper me.

This is a dangerous trap. Rather than renewing our minds, we're falling right into the trap of the worries of the world and the deceitfulness of riches. If we remember the Parable of the Sower, this is the last obstacle that prevented the thirty, sixty, and hundredfold return. There's a sense in which we trust God. Of course we do. If we're Christians, then we say we trust God. But too often our actions reveal that what we really trust is our bank accounts. If we spend the majority of our time and focus on building up resources for our enjoyment and our safety, what does that tell us about whether we're serving God or Mammon?

When we spend all our energy and efforts hedging against risk, hedging against inflation, hedging against this, hedging against that, our entire life becomes a hedge. There's the possibility that the faith we declare might only be a ticket to the afterlife. If we doubt the promises of God so severely that we place all our trust in our own ability to manage risk, then it's possible we may not believe in what God has actually promised us.

This may sound accusatory, but what I'm saying here causes me just as much discomfort as you may be feeling now. What I want to do is encourage both of us to spend time on our knees asking God to search our hearts and show us where and how our investments might better serve him. To do anything else would be too risky. This isn't to scare you into taking risks for God. This is an invitation to share in the full experience of knowing and loving our Savior, Creator God. When we avoid risk, we often end up avoiding what God is doing in the world.

For example, the vast majority of US charitable giving stays within the borders of America. If the vast majority of financial and spiritual poverty is overseas, shouldn't we, as Christ-followers, step into that as an opportunity to make Christ known through our investments? It might seem risky to make investments in entrepreneurs in developing markets, but isn't it even riskier to avoid asking God if that's what he would have us do? We're missing out on the global work of

God! We're living our lives in black and white when they could be technicolor. We could be experiencing the beautiful mosaic that is the body of Christ and every tribe and every nation that exists within it. It's so easy for risk avoidance to become Kingdom avoidance.

The questions we have to ask ourselves are, what are we hedging against? What is it that makes us deem something as risky and therefore worth avoiding? When I started asking myself these questions, it quickly became clear to me that while I said I trusted in God, my investments showed a heart that was hedging against what God could have me do.

A few years ago, an entrepreneur contacted me and wanted to share about his company. He told me that he had a real estate company in Moldova. Immediately, my first thought was that he had contacted the wrong person. I'm not sure how to calculate a cap rate, and at the time I wasn't even sure that Moldova was a country. We talked, and after hearing his pitch, I politely told him that we couldn't invest in what he was doing. It seemed like a no-brainer.

The entrepreneur thanked me for my time, but before he let me go, he asked if I would set up more time with him to help him understand what it meant to be a Faith Driven Entrepreneur. He knew my background and knew that faith was important to me, so much so that he still wanted to talk, regardless of whether that meant he received money from me. He shared that because Moldova was a new country, there wasn't much of a legacy of Faith Driven Entrepreneurs, and he was desperate to learn from somebody.

Just moments before that, I had all but written this phone call off. I wasn't interested, and frankly, I had only agreed to talk with him out of obligation. Now I realized that my own callousness had almost caused me to miss out on what God was doing in a country halfway around the world from me. The result of that conversation and the few I shared with this entrepreneur afterward was the Faith Driven Entrepreneur website, blog, and podcast, which God is now using to reach entrepreneurs all around the world.

I almost missed an invitation by God to see what he is doing in the world. There are companies that make redemptive products and services, leaders that bear witness to the King, all of which advances his Kingdom. Yes, by all stretches it may seem risky to make investments in Christ-following entrepreneurs in frontier markets where entrepreneurial success can have an outsized impact in both the marketplace and culture. There's political risk, currency devaluation, potential corruption, and more to offset the upside of investing. But when a Christ-follower looks at frontier investing as a means to invest in places where there is both financial and spiritual poverty and an outsized ability to make an impact for God's Kingdom, it is riskier not to pray about investing there.

Perhaps a better ending to that story would have been that I ended up taking a huge risk, invested in this entrepreneur, and profited millions of dollars. But that's not what happened. What happened is I caught myself ignoring what God was doing in the world and what he was inviting me to be a part of. From then on, my perspective on what made something risky completely changed.

RISKY BUT NOT RECKLESS

If it sounds like I'm encouraging you to empty your retirement account and invest in an entrepreneur you barely know in a country you can't find on a map, know that's not what I'm saying. I'm not here to be prescriptive. What I want to challenge us on is our heart posture. Are we on our knees daily asking God what we should do with his money? Are we asking him to show us the places in our lives where we're playing it too safe? Are we begging for our eyes to be opened to opportunities to be a part of his work in the world?

My answer to those questions isn't always yes. But my faith in a God who works all things together for good requires that I have a hopeful expectancy that he will use the capital he has placed in my hands in a way that will advance his Kingdom here on earth. That's who God is. That's what he does.

Whether investing or giving, I don't want to encourage you to recklessly throw money at projects and just hope something good comes of it. There's still wisdom and discernment required in all things. Keep in mind that the very process of stepping out to make investments with wisdom brings us into a relationship with others who are trying to accomplish the same mission. This is the community God is calling us toward.

Absent God speaking directly to a person, it's most likely reckless to make a risky frontier investment by yourself. But there is a process of seeking counsel from advisors and peers, both at home and abroad, that keeps God at the forefront. Finding other Christ-followers who are seeking to make wise investments, as well as reaching out to those who may know the unfamiliar market, broadens our understanding of what God is doing and allows us to participate in his work. Yes, that can be messy. Yes, it's time-consuming. But it's so much richer.

I invite you to see that God may have more in mind than just helping you hedge against inflation and save for retirement. We have to ask ourselves: Do we really believe that? Do we really believe that God is working in and through the faithful investments of his people? Do we really believe that he will take care of us? Do we really believe that he's in complete control over all the money and markets in the world? Do we really believe that every investment has an impact?

A lot of people know the power of compounding interest is amazing. Albert Einstein is reported to have said that the power of compounding interest was the most incredible force he'd ever seen. And so some people say, "If I just leave my money in an investment account to compound, then over time, I'll have more to give away." What we're not thinking about is the opposite side of this equation.

If there is a school in Zambia that could be educating four hundred people, but because so many people have chosen to wait for their dollars to compound, they're only able to educate two hundred people, we're missing an opportunity. Their limitations then compound negatively while our money sits in a bank account and grows. There is compounded return on the other side of the equation as well, which asks, what does it look like for those two hundred families who were not served over those seven years? And what is compounded there as well? If we see the good that needs to be done and do not do it, it is sin to us.[1] That is the Word of God. It is more powerful than compound interest.

The application here is not to move all your investments into higher-risk categories. The application is to open up God's Word and spend time in prayer. The scary truth is that those two things may be the riskiest things you ever do, because you don't know what God is going to ask of you. It's scary, and it's exciting. So much is happening in the world because of the faithful stewardship of men and women who are willing to ask God what he would have them do with their money.

It's not reckless, but it is risky. Yet at the same time, the greater risk is in trying to keep God out of your financial decisions and hoping that he won't have something to say about that when you finally see him.

Faith Driven Investors love to talk about the Parable of the Talents. We all have thoughts and ideas for how this specific story Jesus told should inform our investments. But I'd invite you to consider the servant who buried his talent. Think about what his life looked like every day after that.

Not only did he totally miss the master's assignment, but you have to imagine that he lived in pure dread of the master's return. He hadn't asked the master what to do with the money, and he hadn't sought counsel. He just buried it and waited. And every day he looked out of his window with a pit in his stomach, scared to death that he may have done the wrong thing.

Faith Driven Investors shouldn't live in fear. We should know that our master is coming back, and we should be excited about his return. When we open ourselves to take the risks that God would call us to, not only are we preparing ourselves for Judgment Day, but we're also getting to experience and enjoy the excitement of doing God's work today.

The flipside of the Parable of the Talents is the two servants who got to watch their master's money grow. Think of the joy! Think of the anticipation they experienced, eager to share their success with the master when he returned. We can live like that.

What is risk avoidance holding you back from? What is God doing in the world that you're missing out on? How could God use the money you have right now to serve and love his people, both in your own backyard and around the world?

Those are risky questions to ask because they may require you to take some risks. But the riskiest thing we can do is play it safe. Pray and seek the will of God. And open up your heart and mind to the fact that he may have something incredible in store for you—if you're willing to take the risk.

CHAPTER 10

SEEK COLLABORATIVE COMMUNITY

Will Thomas

You could point to a lot of moments that led to the start of Ambassadors Impact Network. One that stands out in particular, however, happened during the Q&A portion of a panel where I was one of the speakers. A member of a family office asked, "How do I find direct investment opportunities where I can not only invest in entrepreneurs but be inspired by the work they're doing?" My response at the time was that unless she wanted to invest an inordinate amount of time sourcing and vetting deals, she should consider investing in a venture fund, even if a fund structure reduced direct connection with entrepreneurs. But after the panel, that question set in motion a series of thoughts that led me to found an organization that enables investors to efficiently source deals, share diligence, and fund companies via a community of like-minded investors.

This family office professional's question highlighted the challenge of finding the investment opportunities that many Faith Driven Investors are seeking. Private investing is time-consuming and demanding in its own right, but it's even more so when potential companies span geographies and industries and seek to make a spiritual and social impact. The effort takes time and deep connections with other investors and entrepreneurs. But the joy of deploying capital that gives rise to a new technology or solution, the satisfaction of creating sustainable and living-wage jobs, and the meaning of giving wings to an entrepreneur's passion to show and share the love of Jesus is worth it.

The question often is simply, how do I get started? How would *you* get started if the Lord called you to invest tens of thousands, or even hundreds of thousands, in Faith Driven Entrepreneurs? Where would you go to find the companies? How would you separate the many seeking capital from the few in which you would want to invest? And how would you support the entrepreneurs through the challenges of growing a company despite business and societal headwinds?

It's difficult to successfully make these investment decisions alone. And it's even more difficult when the considerations are not just along the lines of financial return but also under the weight of making a spiritual and social impact. Effective deployment of capital is best done alongside others with complementary skills and experiences, for sure. Maybe you have the exact entrepreneurs in mind who could use that money to do something good while also making a good return. Or maybe you know someone who knows someone. Either way, your best chance for success is dependent on your ability to coordinate and cooperate with other people. This coordination with others becomes even more critical as you consider the faith-driven aspect of investing. Finding those who share the same passion, think the same way about Faith Driven Investing, and share similar goals is critical.

This idea isn't new. Solomon tells us in Ecclesiastes 4:9 that "Two are better than one, because they have a good return for their labor." In his Gospel, Luke tells us that when Jesus sent the disciples into towns, he sent them in pairs. And of course, there are countless verses throughout Paul's letters explaining the importance of community and connectedness and relying on the strengths of others. All these harken to Proverbs 15:22, where we read, "Plans fail for lack of counsel, but with many advisors they succeed," as well as Proverbs 11:14: "Where there is no guidance, a people falls, but in an abundance of counselors there is safety" (ESV).

In fact, when we think about the Christian life, there isn't a single part of it that is meant to be done alone. We're even instructed that the confession of sins, something we think might be reserved for just us and God, is something we should do with one another.[1] But what about thoughtfully investing our money? Perhaps given the relative taboo nature of this subject even in Christian circles, we should be all the more intentional about seeking others with whom we invest our capital. It is in partnership with others that I have refined what is within limits and what is off limits with respect to my investments. It is in partnership that I've wrestled through what is an adequate financial return. It is in fellowship with others that I've weighed what constitutes sufficient spiritual and social impact.

The Christian life is inherently communal. If we want our faith to drive everything we do, then the same should be true of our investments. I'm not necessarily making an argument for transparency and accountability—though those are important. Instead, I'm sharing the blessing that cooperation and collaboration have been for me as I've worked toward defining and investing along shared goals in fellowship with others.

Investing alongside community hasn't always been the way I've operated. But it is today, and it's made all the difference in the world.

ONE ON ONE

There's more to interacting with entrepreneurs than just dollars and cents. We may know this idea intuitively, but it wasn't until I experienced it in close proximity that I really understood what that meant. Through a ministry called Marketplace Chaplains, I saw how chaplains engaged employees and CEOs by encouraging them in both their professional and their spiritual lives. As I served on the board of a company that had chaplains in place, I started to see how spiritual growth could happen in the context of a workplace.

It's very difficult for people to come to work and leave a part of themselves behind. Everyone, whether they know it or not, has some element of a spiritual life, and that part of themselves follows them to work. As I learned this for myself, my passion grew to see the gospel bless people at work in a contextually appropriate way and that they might hear it accurately and see it lived out well. I saw investing as an opportunity to pursue that goal.

Originally, my faith-driven investment activity began with a company in Haiti. I've had a heart for that country ever since I had flown into Port-au-Prince with the Air Force years ago and seen the depth of that country's poverty. First, I invested in a cement block building company led by an entrepreneur who helped locals escape the stranglehold of voodoo and other similar practices that afflicted their lives and livelihoods.

Soon thereafter, I met an Ethiopian gentleman ten years my senior at a local Bible study. He was a taxi driver, laboring under the expense of renting his taxi, and he wanted to become a driver for Uber Black. To get started, he needed a loan for a late-model black SUV required by the service. So I made the loan, enabling him to buy the car, and began to meet with him monthly for mutual encouragement and so that he could pay me back.

Over the course of our meetings, we shared spiritual insights and eventually joined another Bible study at a local church that helped deepen our relationship with the Lord. Eventually, he paid every dollar of the loan back. Through our meetings and this Bible study, I learned more about his spiritual life and about a raw faith to which I was a foreigner. Through him, I gained a new perspective on the power of Christ, the sustenance found in faith, and the challenges of being an immigrant. We became friends and remain close today.

This experience on the "front lines" of entrepreneurship gave me an impassioned desire to invest in entrepreneurs and their private companies, giving me a front-row seat to the same passion, drive, and life of other entrepreneurs. Given the way the Lord was at work in the company in Haiti and the life of my Ethiopian friend, I began investing in companies whose entrepreneurs were making a social impact with a passion for showing and sharing the love of Jesus. Any entrepreneur who was seeking to love God and share the love of Christ with others was a potential investment. As it turns out, I wasn't the only one with this idea!

THE STORY OF AMBASSADORS IMPACT NETWORK (AIN)

Ambassadors Impact Network was based on a simple idea. A few of us wanted to help connect Faith Driven Investors with gospel-advancing entrepreneurs. My cofounders—Eliot Kerlin and J. J. Barto—and I understand that the entrepreneurial journey is difficult. It's not easy for entrepreneurs to find investors who share their passion for spiritual impact. As Eliot, J. J., and I realized we shared similar passions and interest for funding gospel-advancing entrepreneurs, we discussed with others in our local area about a potential network that would provide education to investors, as well as enable sharing of diligence and deal flow. Once we defined a clear investment mandate, the concept struck a chord.

We began to flesh out the concept of a later-stage angel investment network that would educate, encourage, and enable investors to collaborate in investing in gospel-advancing entrepreneurs. Since our founding in 2018, Ambassadors Impact Network members have funded over twenty-five companies and venture funds with more than $14 million in growth capital.

While the mutual education and investment activity was the initial draw, one of the most compelling aspects of membership became the sense of community we've developed. Perhaps unsurprisingly, when men and women join together around a shared ideological passion into which they are willing to invest time, talent, and treasure, deep bonds of kinship are formed. Much like we encourage entrepreneurs to live their lives in community, by vetting opportunities and investing together, members of the network benefit from the kinship of pressing forward toward a shared goal of spiritual impact.

At first, everything felt simple: it was just Eliot, J. J., and me talking, socializing, and asking others in our circles if they found this or that business of interest. Today, AIN is a group of over fifty Kingdom-minded investors with combined experience of more than 590 years in private investing and over 780 private investments made. But the most catalytic and important part of our growth was to define what our investment criteria would be. If too broad, then it would lack ideological differentiation from other investment efforts. If too narrow or concessionary on returns, the network could yield too little activity to be of interest to potential members. In a series of roundtable discussions with family offices and prospective members, we determined our scope from a spiritual impact and financial return perspective. Our charter members were instrumental in defining AIN's investment criteria.

First, we created a rubric for assessing the spiritual impact of a company by focusing on three areas: documented values, the activities of the company, and the company's products/ services. By being clear about how we would measure spiritual impact, we figured we could best protect against mission drift and fund companies that were best able to bless all peoples spiritually. Our desire is *not* to prescribe what a company should be doing to achieve spiritual impact. Instead, we work to understand how the entrepreneur is showing and sharing Jesus given his or her particular gifting, context, and passion. They usually answer these questions about how they think about spiritual impact via their funding application.

The questions are straightforward. How is God using your business? How do you see your work as an opportunity to bless others? We ask about their operating principles and whether those principles are biblically and theologically aligned with what we believe, and we let them expound on that. We also ask them about their activities internally that allow people to see or hear the gospel at work. And then we ask whether the products or services themselves advance the gospel in some way, either by demonstration or proclamation.

So it's these three areas—the documents, the activities, and the products or services themselves—that we assess to see if an investment is a fit. We also want to be well-matched with the other investors and the directors. Understanding all the people who are in leadership of the company is important to us to make sure we're congruent with them.

We recognize that investments led by those with other or no faith convictions have and do generate significant financial returns with great social impact. But that's not where we feel called to invest. Almost every other angel network and financial investment platform facilitates the funding of businesses led without respect to the faith of the business leaders. We want to provide something different.

Our experience indicates that Christian entrepreneurs who boldly live out their faith run into roadblocks from investors, not to mention that these entrepreneurs face unique challenges as they seek to balance profit, business excellence, God's environmental mandate, and Jesus' example of care. We want to step into that challenge and help.

We also defined the minimum financial return we would consider. In short, we agreed to consider investments in companies that demonstrated a rate of return equivalent to half of the market rate of return of a comparable company. In other words, if a typical angel investor would want to see a 30 percent internal rate of return (IRR) from a company with this risk profile, we'd consider investing as long as our estimated IRR was at least 15 percent. In short, we believed that to have adequate deal flow for the spiritual impact we were seeking, we would need to take a greater risk (or accept less return, which is the other side of that same coin). Once our investment criteria were clearly defined, it allowed potential members to clearly understand whether we were a fit for them or not. It saved a lot of time and fast-tracked conversations, as there are many places for members to spend their time looking for faith-driven companies. In our case, once we defined the specific niche of entrepreneurs we were looking for, more investors than we expected were interested in this niche.

Ultimately, our mission is to properly steward the capital God has provided with wisdom and purpose to enable Faith Driven Entrepreneurs to accomplish their God-given missions. Recognizing that many family offices and accredited investors have limited time to devote to diligence and post-investment activity, we seek to leverage their time and make decision-making and knowledge-sharing as efficient as possible. Our aim is to provide a service to both entrepreneurs and investors: entrepreneurs who are seeking like-minded investors, and investors seeking to fund gospel-advancing entrepreneurs. We help both parties connect efficiently.

HOW AIN WORKS

Like any functioning organization, AIN has a specific cadence to its activity. Our activities generally fall into serving members, seeking companies to fund, and serving our portfolio companies. To organize all this, we have a weekly call with the directors and chief operating officer of AIN. Our time begins with prayer for our members, portfolio companies, prospective companies, and whatever else the Lord puts on our hearts. We consider upcoming member meetings, various educational opportunities, and new initiatives.

Our members are served most frequently through a weekly update that includes prospective companies, educational content, and community news. This gives members the ability to dig into the companies, participate in diligence, and get to know each other. We also host quarterly member meetings, which began as in-person-only events but now are hybrid, allowing members from across the country to join. During these events, we have pitches from prospective companies; a network update detailing recent activity, spiritual impact, and financial returns; and time for in-person members to connect over a meal. We also have regular meetings with our limited set of "young professionals" who are non-accredited private equity professional members. These "young pros" are the backbone of much of our work and benefit from working alongside accredited members in seeing a deal come to fruition.

To find fitting companies, we keep active in the faith-driven, redemptive, and business-as-mission ecosystems. It's a joy to have such great partners across so many formal organizations, informal organizations, like-minded event coordinators, funds, family offices, investors, and advisors. Our members travel nationwide to speak on panels and provide interviews. Many of them are direct sources for potential investments. Once a potentially fitting company expresses interest in funding, we invite them to apply via a clearly defined process that seeks to get them a clear answer regarding a fit in short order.

Once we've invested in a portfolio company, we have a defined process of impact reporting and prayer support. Each company that receives funding from AIN agrees to participate in our quarterly/semiannual reporting process. Most are greatly encouraged by the opportunity to report on what the Lord is doing through their business. And our close relationship enables us to be a support in times of need, including personnel changes, additional fundraising efforts, and strategic decisions.

At times our members serve on the board or as advisors of the company. We always have at least one accredited member serve as a liaison who offers encouragement and prayer support to the company. We're looking to provide entrepreneurs with three things: capital, counsel, and connectedness. This sounds simple, and frankly, kind of obvious, but in order to do all three well, it's about building trust—that includes in the entrepreneur-investor relationship and between our group of investors. We can't invest in entrepreneurs and tell them we're interested in their whole person—body, mind, and soul—while neglecting one another. Otherwise, we're just writing checks together, hoping to turn a profit, and there's nothing deeper going on. Instead, what we're doing is aligning on very real spiritual goals and then working together to see those ideas become reality.

A point of clarification: AIN is not a broker or a fund. We are a 501(c)(6) business association to whom members pay annual dues, but AIN does not otherwise charge fees. AIN is not a venture fund and does not invest its own capital.

AIN doesn't recommend investments. It is an educational and knowledge-sharing platform. Any and all investment decisions are made by AIN members on an individual basis, which allows funds to be invested directly by the investor and go back to the investor after they exit the investment.

Ultimately, the most impactful way we see God's people doing amazing things is by working together as a group. This is especially true in the context of Faith Driven Investing. Are there investments we disagree on? Of course. Does that mean we just give up and go our separate ways? No. We believe in iron sharpening iron. We believe in working together as the body of Christ.

This is how God works and moves in and through his people. There's nothing more fulfilling than working with others to be a conduit for what God hopes to accomplish in the world. Frankly, it's something I can't do on my own. Thankfully, I don't have to. My hope for you is that you find your group of like-minded investors, whether it is AIN or another group that fits the passion the Lord has given you.

CHAPTER 11

WORK LOCALLY AND GLOBALLY

Efosa Ojomo and Richard Okello

One evening, Jesus and his disciples were spotted having dinner with a whole bunch of sinners and tax collectors. When the Pharisees confronted his disciples about their conspicuously bad decision to fellowship with "bad people," Jesus said to them, "It is not the healthy who need a doctor, but the sick. . . . I have not come to call the righteous, but sinners."[1] And just like that, what seemed to be a bad decision took on new meaning. What a difference a simple change in perspective can make!

Similarly, investing time or treasure in anything can also be a paradox. True investing seeks to create goodness, wealth, and value from places where there is little, and in some cases, where there is nothing. However, paradoxically, our starting point as investors is usually one of great comfort with what we already know to be good and of discomfort with the unknown. That can create a perspective that leads to inaction. Good investors see potential and opportunity where others may only see problems. Faith Driven Investors, often motivated by their beliefs and the opportunity to create value for others, can be a powerful force for good in a world that so desperately needs it. To activate that force for good, though, often we need to change our perspective.

Eight years from now (by 2030), there will be more than 1.6 billion potential customers in Africa, a number greater than the projected population of Europe and the United States combined or even the total population of China![2] Half of these consumers will live in cities that are growing at unprecedented rates and will need everything that we may take for granted—groceries, schools, electricity, water, health services, wireless internet, and so on.

That said, the deluge of bad news that the global news media focuses on creates a lot of noise. And it can be near impossible to pierce through this noise and see the enormous potential that this fast-evolving landscape offers for investors to create goodness, wealth, and value. This is not just an African phenomenon but rather a global one. We could say the same about neighborhoods close to us that we are not as familiar with or that we perceive as narrowly representing more problems than opportunity or potential. By changing our perspectives, we can more clearly see the unique opportunity that places like Africa offer us as Faith Driven Investors and Faith Driven Entrepreneurs to create value for billions of people.

There are, however, three massive misconceptions that need to be corrected before we can see this value creation happen on a global scale. The first is that many churchgoing Americans and people of other faiths around the world think of Africa and other emerging or frontier economies as places that are primarily in need of philanthropic support. Yes, charitable giving can be impactful, but active investments and profitable businesses (alongside addressing other systemic issues) are what will make a self-sustaining difference in those economies and enable emerging economies to begin to solve global problems.

The second misconception is much like the first—narrowness of perspective. Investing in places such as Africa or Latin America is not just about microfinance. It is multifaceted in nature and incredibly varied in scale. Small, early-stage, or venture capital investments in Fora, which began as a distance learning platform for African Universities in 2013 based in Nigeria, West Africa, have evolved into Andela, a global programming talent platform serving over two hundred companies around the world. More sizable, private-equity investments alongside trusted partners can support well-run companies that are constrained by capital availability to scale even more (and by doing so create quality jobs and expand access to affordable food, electricity, and healthcare). Faith Driven Investors who are also debt providers can find numerous opportunities at different levels of magnitude to increase access to credit through established private credit institutions. The list goes on.

The third misconception is that such regions lack appropriate institutions to safeguard the value that is created or are just too difficult to navigate. Again, a change in perspective may help here. We must ask ourselves how it is that close to half of the top fifty companies in the world, including household names such as Walmart and Apple, actively invest in Africa and have done so for years. They have spent time understanding the opportunity and finding the right partners to work with. They have focused on countries with strong institutional backdrops and learned what things to avoid. Many of these companies are not primarily motivated by the conviction of their faith to create sustained impact. Imagine what a Faith Driven Investor who also understands the broader economic impact that is possible can accomplish in areas that others might consider to be impossible!

It's time for us to see the whole picture.

WHY THIS MATTERS NOW

Before the COVID-19 pandemic wreaked havoc across the globe, extreme poverty had been declining rapidly. Only 9 percent of the global population lived on less than $1.90 a day ($693 annually, the threshold for extreme poverty). When the pandemic struck, wealthy economies provided billions of dollars in relief and stimulus checks to their citizens, which helped cushion losses in income.

By comparison, poorer economies spent significantly less and required their citizens to shelter in place with little or nothing to offset the negative income impact of reduced mobility. In countries like Honduras, the pandemic was followed by natural disasters that left tens of thousands homeless. In the East African region, swarms of locusts exacerbated an already difficult harvesting season that led to massive food shortages on the continent. In fact, all things considered, the fact that emerging and frontier economies had a modest decline (relative to what many had expected) reflects a resilience that is nothing short of remarkable.

That said, since the onset of the pandemic, economists estimate that around 100 million people will slide into extreme poverty. Many businesses and communities that were growing rapidly slowed or reversed course, which has impacted their abilities to create redemptive wealth and value for ordinary people. While this might signal doom and gloom for the average reader, Faith Driven Investors can and should see a redemptive opportunity. By investing in solving these problems, Faith Driven Investors can not only help people but also generate returns, create wealth, and unlock value for the world.

There are no easy solutions to the many problems the world faces. But for the Faith Driven Investor, there is a template. Just like Jesus, who sought out those whom society had cast out, the Faith Driven Investor must equally seek to invest in places where there seems to be little to no opportunity, at least on the surface. They must look beyond the obvious challenges to see the incredible opportunity. It is not until we change the lens with which we assess opportunities that we will begin to see and act differently.

Now, keep in mind that investing in frontier markets (whether in Africa, Asia, Europe, or anywhere else) is completely different from investing in developed markets. Investing in developed countries comes with larger, more efficient, and more organized markets. The types of opportunities and risks you have in those markets are very different from the ones in emerging or frontier regions such as Africa. For many involved in developed market private equity, the focus is finding investors with highly specialized skills who focus on squeezing out the last remaining efficiencies in a business in order to generate returns.

If you were to take that private equity mindset to Africa, it would be a disaster. For example, middle-market businesses in the United States typically grow at 8 to 12 percent a year, whereas in Africa, businesses grow at 20, 30, 40, 50, or even 100 percent a year. Businesses growing that quickly generally have simple business models that are being overwhelmed by rising demand. They typically lack appropriately structured financing and the management breadth required for their current growth, and they may be challenged in their regional or cross-border expansion. Addressing those challenges can support or accelerate growth and deliver substantial impact, even though certain minor inefficiencies might still exist. It was these sorts of opportunities to generate return alongside scalable, sustained impact that attracted me (Richard) to making private investments in Africa.

In Kenya, for example, something as simple as large-scale, organized, and reliable pharmacy chains—things we take for granted in the United States with CVS Pharmacy or in Europe with Boots—were missing. Instead, lots of individuals owned one, two, or three pharmacy shops in select cities. Although there was a prevailing medical regulatory process and law, inadequate enforcement meant that consumers were constantly checking whether the medications they obtained were authentic.

We partnered with a local team to acquire an initial three stores, created a common brand with appropriate quality control, and scaled up that business. In that way, Goodlife Pharmacy was born and precipitated a similar wave across other brands beyond Kenya and into neighboring countries. That investment required a different perspective, the right capital, and expanded management expertise. We combined these things, and the investment was acquired from the early investors for an attractive return in less than three years.

Although these business requirements sound like simple things, the return and social impact you can generate through local businesses like this all across Africa are unprecedented. This business alone has impacted healthcare for over a million city dwellers. It created over four hundred quality jobs across over ninety stores in two countries and won the prestigious World Brand Award (Healthcare-Pharmacies category) in 2020–2021. Africa is one of those rare places where you can find massive growth and massive impact in the same business.

Another example of a high-growth, high-return, and high-impact investment opportunity is organized grocery retail. The first organized grocery business in the United States was Piggly Wiggly, which began in 1916 in Memphis, Tennessee, at a time when the US population was around one hundred million people and the largest city (New York) had roughly five million. Fast-forward a hundred years, and look at Nigeria. In 2015, Nigeria was home to nearly two hundred million people (twice the population of the US in 1916), and Lagos, the largest city in Nigeria, had twenty million people, four times that of New York in 1916. Yet in 2015, Nigeria had only fifteen grocery stores. That's it!

Compare that to Brazil, whose population is similar to that of Nigeria. In 2015 Brazil had 2,200 grocery stores. Therein lies the opportunity and the challenge. People's behavior is not that different. In the United States, Brazil, and Nigeria, people want to go to a grocery store that's organized, get what they want, know that it's fresh and reliable, find it at a good price, and take it home to their families. It's not a complicated problem.

In 2015, after looking at the sector for some time, my team at Sango Capital backed an entrepreneur to build out a grocery store chain providing ordinary items to ordinary people, reliably and affordably. Six years later, Marketsquare is a twenty-store grocery chain employing over 1,400 people. It provides fresh food and dry goods at prices ordinary Nigerians can afford. It saves locals time that would otherwise be spent battling traffic to get to informal food markets, allowing parents to spend more time in their homes with their families. It has been built through what many would describe as challenging times, as Nigeria's economy underwent a recession and foreign currency pressures, among other things. But that business is already delivering outstanding performance. That's another example of the type of place where Faith Driven Investors can make a difference.

IT ONLY TAKES TWO RULES

Let's return where we began with a story from God's Word.

There's a story in the Gospel of Matthew where a Pharisee lawyer asks Jesus the following question: "Which is the greatest commandment in the Law?"[3] His goal wasn't to learn what the greatest commandment was and how he might orient his life toward it. It was to stump Jesus.

See, there were 613 Jewish commandments that devoted Jews had to follow. It was a heavy burden, but the Pharisees had somehow figured out how to follow so many laws that they were considered the holy ones. In addition to being burdensome, following the laws cultivated a spirit of pride. So Jesus came to give them, and the many others who would abide in him, rest. He simplified the 613 laws into two.

Love God. Love people. That's it. Everything else is background noise.

For people used to engaging in so much religious activity, hearing that must have been difficult. But for those who were truly looking to abide in God, help their neighbors, and surrender all to him, it was indeed good news.

Those who found rest in the words of Christ understood they could spend their whole lives trying to obey the 613 Jewish laws and still lead miserable lives. Jesus helped them see that obeying the laws was never the goal. It was supposed to lead them—to lead us all—to God. By falling short, we would be reminded of God's grace.

For how could the greatest commandment, according to Jesus, be for us to love God and others if Jesus wasn't the personification of love itself? It's paradoxical, but by focusing on love, we inadvertently accomplish the other laws.

Love supersedes the 613.

Similarly, when it comes to fighting poverty, contributing meaningfully to positive, values-based change, or helping accelerate local solutions that are already working well, faith-driven professionals—investors, entrepreneurs, and philanthropists—need a different lens. We can go into poor communities and build wells, schools, and healthcare facilities. But much like the 613 laws, waking up every day and striving to provide water, schools, and hospitals is burdensome and difficult to sustain without our continued involvement. How many well-meaning Christian mission trips to build things have we funded? How many can we say have led to sustainable economic and financial impact in the lives of the people we went to serve? Most people who were poor when we started investing in their lives remain poor today.

Unfortunately, too many of these projects focus on the symptoms of a deeper problem and not the root cause. This happened to me (Efosa) when I started Poverty Stops Here (PSH). Through the help of many friends and members of my church family at the time, PSH built wells in communities and provided funding for schools. But much of what we uilt didn't last. The wells broke, the schools were subpar, and sustainability was hard to come by. Through the process, however, we learned.

We were not building the mechanism that helps societies eradicate poverty and ultimately prosper. That mechanism is innovation.

But not just any kind of innovation—market-creating innovations. These innovations are unique in their ability to transform complicated and expensive products into simple and affordable products so more people in society can afford them. When investors and entrepreneurs build market-creating innovations, they provide a foundation for robust economic growth. They provide jobs and taxes, and they can lead a cultural revolution that highlights the importance of innovation and entrepreneurship.

For example, when Henry Ford innovated with the Model T, he made cars (and mobility) affordable to a whole range of people who historically couldn't afford them. As a result, he created hundreds of thousands of jobs and changed the landscape of the United States and the world. Many other entrepreneurs believed they too could create affordable cars and thus an industry was born.

The mechanism to help people move around more easily was the Model T, a market-creating innovation.

When faith-driven professionals focus on market-creating innovation, they have even more of an opportunity to significantly change the culture in a country. By building market-creating companies, they can influence so many people—from their employees to the customers they serve—with the love Jesus spoke about, and subsequently, influence culture. Their influence is more likely to last because the organizations they create will last.

Jesus helped the Pharisee lawyer see that focusing on love was the greatest commandment. Love, in many ways, transcended all the laws one could follow. For faith-driven professionals looking to eradicate poverty and suffering in the world, innovation is the mechanism. We can do a world of good by getting the mechanism right.

None of this, of course, is easy. Investing internationally requires an intense number of hours. It requires having people in your local network in the places where you're directing capital while also spending as much time as you can talking to those same people in person. Technology has advanced to where we can have video calls, but we still haven't replaced the importance of meeting in person.

Few things are more effective than going to the place where someone lives and seeing what they do on a daily basis. Yes, things like 360-degree cross-referencing and talking to people in their network (including their competitors, their lawyers, their auditors and accounts, the local government authority, and others) are all helpful. But you can't beat showing up in person.

Several years ago, I (Richard) was conducting due diligence on a group that argued their integrity was driven by their Christian faith. So I flew out to their country and went to two of their churches unannounced. I just attended the church and asked around about these people. They were shocked I had come all that way just to learn about them, but I got a much better sense talking to others in the community for who these people were in practice than I would have just running a remote due diligence operation in the background.

That's where Faith Driven Investors can thrive. We can work locally and globally at the same time. We can enter into the spaces where growth is happening, understand what's really working well within a local context, and bear witness to a community-minded approach that is built upon the same love that Jesus told us to share with the world.

Global investments may sound like a large and audacious idea. But when we take a local approach to different countries and continents, we get to see that the work God is doing is happening not just in our own backyard, but in every backyard around the world.

CHAPTER 12

VIEW INVESTMENTS AS PARTNERSHIPS

Jessica Kim

If you asked people to tell you the goal of a startup, most would say it's to make money, solve problems, innovate, or make the world a better place. And yes, those things are true and legitimate goals. As believers, though, in everything we do, our goal is rooted in the two greatest commandments: first, to love God with all our heart, with all our soul, with all our mind, and with all our strength. The second is to love our neighbors as we love ourselves.

So for years, I've been thinking—what would the startup journey look like if the main goal of the founder and the investors was to love people? Few people would define the entrepreneur-investor relationship as one of love. Typically, at its core, it's a transactional relationship. Entrepreneurs are building products or services to serve their customers. Investors ultimately want a return on their investment. At any one moment, entrepreneurs and investors may feel aligned. However, when our relationships are based on the value of the transaction, it is likely that the entrepreneur and investor will be on completely different sides at some point because they are driven by different goals. This difference is the root of misaligned expectations, which cause tension, games, and dishonesty.

I believe there's a better way.

FROM BAKING BANANA BREAD TO SUPPORTING CAREGIVERS

I'm the cofounder and CEO of my third startup. Each venture was backed by investors ranging from angel investors to venture capital. My perspective on the entrepreneur-investor relationship has progressed as my understanding of redemptive entrepreneurship has grown.

As a sophomore in college, I started my first company out of my dorm room. It was a baked goods company called Jessica's Wonders with an unforgettable slogan: "Mmm-hh . . . so good it'll make you wonder." It all started with a random moment when I walked into a local pizzeria and saw some banana bread on sale. It was plastic wrapped with a handmade $1.69 sign on it. I told the owner I could do so much better than what he was selling, and he challenged me to bring something in. I brought my first banana bread loaf in, and he sold out. I brought in more, and he sold out again. Before I knew it, I was selling to all the hotspots around campus. By senior year I ended up raising one million dollars from investors and grew the business to national distribution with several million in revenue. It was an incredible and raw experience. I didn't intend to start a business; I was just a college student majoring in anthropology, trying to figure out what I wanted to be when I grew up.

I was also a new and very eager young Christian. So when I realized I had a thriving business on my hands, I thought the whole purpose was to share my belief in God. I displayed my baked goods in baskets with signs made out of construction paper and markers. Every sign had John 3:16 written out. I'll never forget when the *Wall Street Journal* interviewed a few entrepreneurs and asked us about our favorite business book. People like Bill Gates shared their top-selling leadership titles, and I felt the need to say the Bible. And the *Wall Street Journal* actually printed it!

I laugh now at these examples of my innocence and pure-hearted intentions. The way I expressed being a Christian and an entrepreneur at that time was by slapping verses on products and mentioning my faith at every opportunity. During my second venture, I realized it's more integrated than that. The way I treat my employees and how we impact our customers' lives go beyond the product itself. That has never been as true as it is for my current venture, ianacare, a solution to support family caregivers as they navigate care in the home. My dad and I were thrust into being my mom's full-time caregiver as she battled pancreatic cancer for seven years. As they moved in with me and my family, I was forced to quit my job to become their primary caregiver, managing my mom's medical care, performing the nursing duties, and juggling all the financial and coordination logistics. It was the hardest and loneliest time in my life. After she passed away, in my deep grief, my eyes opened to the 54 million family caregivers in the United States alone who are the invisible backbone of our entire healthcare system and society.

These people are untrained and unsupported family members taking care of loved ones with prolonged illnesses, special needs, disabilities, or aging in their home. They are exhausted, they are desperate, and they feel alone. In this highly emotional state, they need to make tough decisions and spend a lot of money with a lack of direction or transparency. My aha moment was discovering that there are thousands of resources and services that already exist hidden in our local communities, employer and health plan benefits, and even in our own personal social circles. My cofounder, Steve Lee, and I combined our skills and personal experiences as caregivers to create a tech and human solution that organizes and mobilizes all the layers of support needed in the home.

Having found myself in caregivers' shoes and knowing how hard that journey is, empathy came naturally. But it wasn't empathy alone that led me to start ianacare. It was empathy as an expression of love. I had to ask myself, *Am I observing, researching, and trying to understand my end user to make their life better, or to grab an insight into what would lead them to purchase? Is it my intent to acquire them or to care for them?* This intent colors the lens through which I view and interpret their needs and desires, and it shapes what I do with the insights I get.

Making something people want is very different from making something people want that will also lead to their flourishing.

Empathy-driven insight is a proven method to understand consumer needs in order to get them to purchase. If my approach is rooted in empathy alone, I could take advantage of my understanding of people's desperation to create a service that purposely made them dependent on what we offered. I could easily require our service to be the connector. Some would say that's a great business model because we wouldn't be cut out of the transaction. But if I'm driven by leveraging that empathy and understanding to truly love, instead I would create a service that empowered people with all the knowledge they needed to make the best decision for their family—even if it meant they no longer needed us. Building sustainable systems of support is the only way to truly care long term and address the deep isolation that exists.

With both approaches, you could prove through early testing and feedback that caregivers wanted a given service. However, the real test is what happens after the purchase. If your goal is to love, you will take that deep empathetic insight and create the product that allows people to flourish beyond the purchase.

This is the difference between a transactional relationship and a relationship built on love and genuine partnership. It is only possible to truly create a redemptive venture in this way if all people involved are treated as partners. This is especially true of the entrepreneur-investor relationship. Through all three of my ventures, what ended up being a key factor was the fundraising and alignment with investors. I used to think investors were needed just to fund the product and idea, but the funding strategy and investors were either the accelerant or the roadblock to achieving our ultimate mission.

SEEING PEOPLE AS PEOPLE

Love comes down to people.

It's common knowledge that business success is dependent on the people behind it. There are countless books and talks about the importance of management and leadership.

As CEO, I saw firsthand the impact of a leader's personal values, mood, choice of words, and reactions to all the crazy situations that come up. Whether you know it or not, whether you want it or not, who you are and what you do as the leader makes such a difference to your team. Our culture puts so much emphasis on the *power* of leadership. "Take ownership! Be confident! Make clear and tough decisions!" What about *love*? What does it mean to love your team as a leader?

It's common to think of employees as the people you pay to get something done. Especially when I was paying my first team members from my personal savings account, I wanted them to be as dedicated as I was. I wanted them to stay up all night with me and sacrifice their free time. But I soon learned that I don't own them.

Investors can experience something similar. Are the entrepreneurs and businesses in which you have invested capital solely there for your own gain? Are they simply the jockey for the horse you bet on? Do you care about the people in the business as much as the profit they bring you? Are you loving the performance and productivity of your investments? Or are you loving the people on the other side of the money?

It's hard to see people through God's eyes when the relationship is built on performance expectations, but that's exactly what we're called to do. I've learned to see people with a long view and to keep the perspective that our time together is part of a bigger journey. I tell employees, "I don't expect you to work here forever. I know you have your own path and aspirations. You're an important part of this company's vision, but what is your own vision for yourself, and how can I help you get there?" This message is often met with surprise.

One of my product managers said he ultimately wanted to be a business professor, which was not something I would have guessed. That conversation helped me give him opportunities to gain the skills and perspective he needed to move forward in God's path for him. He was one of my most effective teammates.

Frank Chen of Andreessen Horowitz expresses a similar view of investing, what he calls seeing your investor role as a servant leader. So often we think of the relationship between entrepreneur and investor as a constant power struggle, but Frank Chen is upending that idea and offering a much more redemptive and selfless approach.

When I think of how this type of relationship works in my own life, I often think of my second venture's cofounder, Christine. I read somewhere that seven out of ten times, the cofounder relationship can create tremendous stress that ruins a company's potential. So I wanted to be super intentional about this relationship. My cofounder and I made a vow to each other that we would always make sure we were aligned. Our friendship took priority over the possible success of the venture. We asked each other two hundred hard questions to uncover sensitive topics, potential issues, and shared values. Yes, two hundred questions, such as "What if an investor wanted to invest, but only if I fired you?" and "What if we only had money to pay one person?" and "What if one of us started doing unethical things? How would we handle it?" We couldn't predict all situations that would arise, but our transparent conversations aligned our values and mindset so that when those unexpected situations came up—and there were many!—we were ready to face them.

Despite departing the business in its last stages, Christine is one of my closest friends in life, and we're stronger than when we first started the business. Regardless of whether an investment or venture succeeds or fails, what people will remember is how they were treated and how it felt to be part of it.

IS FUNDRAISING BROKEN?

When we talk about things like love and empathy, it's hard to discern where those should come into the fundraising process. But if we want to redeem relationships, specifically those between entrepreneurs and investors, we can start by being transparent about some of the tensions that exist. These unspoken subtleties can create a relationship based on distrust or gamesmanship, whereas the ideal is to find a true partner who shares your desires to create something new and impact the world.

If we ask Faith Driven Entrepreneurs to root themselves in love and purpose, then the same should be said for Faith Driven Investors. Christian investors and entrepreneurs alike should seek to build sustainable ventures that enable people to flourish. Without that partnership, it's almost impossible to achieve our goals. This sounds great on paper, but in practice it's not always that simple.

A big part of the fundraising process is figuring out the size of the opportunity and the expected projections. Is the market big enough? Are you the team I trust to get there? How are you going to do it? Investors want a large market with fast growth. The venture capital business model is typically built on one of an investor's ten investments being the unusual "unicorn." On the other hand, entrepreneurs want to be realistic in their goals and projections because, from our perspective, this is the one venture that is going to impact our personal lives. We don't have a portfolio of options like investors do. This is the one thing we're going all-in on. We have to be practical and realistic with what we can achieve so we can align our day-to-day operations.

But at the same time, there's pressure to show that we're creating a rocket ship. I remember presenting projections for ianacare, and the feedback was, "Well, that's just not big enough. That's not aggressive enough." At the time, I was talking about $40–$50 million in four years, and it still wasn't big enough. I was tempted to stretch those numbers to get the investment, but I knew that would be wrong—not just from a practical perspective but from a relationship-building perspective.

I didn't want investors to get involved with me because they thought they could get something from me that I wasn't sure I could deliver. Still, there's this tension that if you don't present a big enough opportunity, then you might not even get that meeting.

This is where posturing becomes a very real dynamic. On the investor side, FOMO is one of the most influential factors that dictates their actions. Everyone wants to get in on the hot deal, whatever that may be, because they trust the market and it adds credibility to the firm or their reputation. On the entrepreneur side, everyone wants to show that they can be the unicorn. They want to say they're the ones with the unique advantages and the work ethic to crush Red Bulls over their heads as they build the next billion-dollar business. The problem is both parties are posturing to be more interested and bigger than they truly are just for the chance to get a transaction done in the moment.

As an entrepreneur, you can't be someone you're not just to get the deal. As an investor, you can't pretend to care about the mission and vision of an organization when your only goal is street credit and capital. Why not? Because those are foundations built on sand that begin to crack and fall apart as the relationship moves forward.

When an entrepreneur has put on a front just to get an investment, it's only a matter of time before the reality of the situation is found out. And for an investor who is only in it for the money, there eventually comes a time when a personal and relational decision has to be made that will reveal everyone's true colors. Similar to any other part of the operations, funding has to respond and react to overcome roadblocks. If there is no vision or belief in the mission, the approach will be stunted to what was initially expected, and investors will tend to walk away when it veers off track.

But as Faith Driven Investors and Faith Driven Entrepreneurs look to work together, we can address these common tensions in a transparent way to achieve the bigger impact of what we're creating. We can also pursue a relationship where we see the other person as a human being rather than our one chance to get a home run or our vehicle for funding. Ultimately, we can seek true partnership.

BUILDING A REDEMPTIVE PARTNERSHIP

If building a redemptive venture is a shared goal, how do we create a redemptive partnership to achieve that? We're missing out on a lot of amazing opportunities to build incredible redemptive ventures because of the posturing at the beginning of the relationship. We need to let go of that; that's our call. Christians have the opportunity to model how we can avoid the pitfalls and dynamics that tear businesses, investments, and relationships apart.

If you think about it, a lot of the investor-entrepreneur relationship can be compared to the marriage relationship. When you're looking for a spouse, you don't posture and pretend. Or, if you do, you know you're committing to a lifetime of pretending. Instead, both parties should come to the table with honesty and empathy. We should be asking each other questions like, what are we going to build together? Why do we want to build it? Are we aligned on this practice and idea? Where are our boundaries? How do we define success, and how will we act when we experience failure? That's our greatest chance of actually making it succeed.

It comes down to having a partner relationship—a "we're in this together" mentality. As I mentioned earlier, entrepreneurs and investors are coming into the business with two different perspectives. For the entrepreneur, this is their life. It's their one business, the sole thing they've committed their time and energy to. For the investor, this business is only one part of a larger portfolio. Even aligning on something as simple as that can clear up so much confusion. Recognizing the difference in how both parties view this opportunity will clearly communicate what is expected. I love it when investors share their portfolio strategy with me and how my venture fits into it.

It also helps to get aligned on timing expectations. If an entrepreneur is thinking about growing the business over the course of several decades, whereas the investor only plans to stay involved for the next two years, conflict will follow. Being transparent about where the fund is in its life cycle and what drives investor decisions will also help the entrepreneur manage various funding sources. Entrepreneurs have to think about respecting the various models that represent the respective shareholders. Investors, however, only have to prioritize their own goals.

A lack of transparency about what all the parties hope to achieve, as well as an unclear understanding of how each person plans to contribute toward that goal, muddy the waters and make a healthy relationship nearly impossible. Entrepreneurs, then, shouldn't walk into pitches hoping that all investors say yes. They should expect mismatches and look for true partners. Investors shouldn't pretend to be super interested in investing when all they hope for is the "option" for a unicorn. They should look for true partners to build solutions to problems that address their convictions.

Both parties need to be able to look each other in the eye and speak the truth about what's really going on. There needs to be unity around the purpose of the business, empathy toward one another as they work together to meet their goals, and transparency on how they want to do whatever it is they're going to do.

Rarely do these virtues shine through in meetings between entrepreneurs and investors. It's more like a face-off instead of two parties searching for shared convictions, where investors and entrepreneurs play different roles but both with the goal of making an impact.

It takes both entrepreneurs and investors to come in with humility, willing to learn from and understand one another. I have experienced incredible partnerships with redemptive investors. We deeply respect each other's roles, we unite when challenges arise, we understand each other's expectations and needs, we openly keep each other accountable, and we genuinely care about each other—all with the intent to move an important mission forward with deep conviction. We strive for financial wins and societal impact, but we both know that God has a greater purpose beyond our own understanding.

If we can enter the relationship with that posture together, the redemptive impact goes beyond the possible business outcome. We actually experience redemption and love in a glorifying way throughout the entire pursuit. That is what's going to make a partnership worth pursuing. A functional entrepreneur-investor relationship is built on love and empathy. With those two virtues underlying every conversation, every decision, every idea, that's when we can build something rooted in our greatest calling—to love.

CHAPTER 13

PULL FROM ONE POCKET

Bryce Butler

On February 25, 1901, U.S. Steel became the world's first official billion-dollar company. It was the dawn of a new era in capitalism that would give rise to the world's first $10 billion, $100 billion, and $1 trillion companies within a little over a century. It was also the dawn of a century that would see both Hiroshima and a polio vaccine, climate change and women's suffrage, and dramatic evolution in the arts, scholarship, culture, and enterprise.

Behind the scenes of the twentieth century's vivid drama, in the middle pages of the *New York Times* business section, new finance and investment theories were evolving as well. Hidden by layers of conceptual and regulatory complexity were ideas that continue to shape our world in deeply powerful ways. The results have not always been positive, perhaps because the ideas themselves were not always approached thoughtfully.

We can no longer afford to be thoughtless in our approach to ideas about finance and investment. Capital drives evolution in global economies as well as in local communities and individual opportunities. But for too long, we have not asked the difficult questions that complex financial systems require, choosing instead to ask easy questions with facile answers. The results have been dire on every front—global, local, and individual. To even begin to meet the world's crises, we have to examine the foundational values of our economic activity—not only to ask what capital management can accomplish, but also to ask what capital management means.

These are difficult questions, but they are questions with exciting and life-giving answers. I intend to examine how investing quietly diverged from values, to explore the growing movement to reunite these concepts, and to introduce a new lens called "one-pocket investing" that integrates investment and values into a single process. The outcomes of this conversation will guide twenty-first-century change in foundational ways.

WHAT THE ONE-POCKET CONVERSATION IS ALL ABOUT

One-pocket investing, the approach that operates with the understanding that organizations and individuals don't have to compromise their missions and values to achieve financial return objectives, is neither a new nor a niche idea. Under various labels, it emerged in the mid-1980s and now influences organizations like the Bill & Melinda Gates Foundation and the Chan Zuckerberg Initiative, not to mention a growing number of capital and wealth specialists like the Caprock Group[1]. Nevertheless, one pocket lacks a clear language and narrative describing what it is and is not. What the Gates Foundation may call a philanthropic venture, the Chan Zuckerberg Initiative will call concessionary funding and Veris Wealth Partners might call values-driven investing.

Three core ideas emerge from these different conversations: resource stewardship, alignment of values with finances, and merging front-pocket profitable investments with back-pocket philanthropy funding. These ideas converge to comprise the one-pocket approach to investing. First defined in 2017 by Ross Baird in *The Innovation Blind Spot*, one-pocket investing is a shift "from two-pocket thinking (a pocket for profits, a pocket for charitable giving) to a one-pocket mindset (investing for both profit and social good)."[2]

HISTORY OF ONE-POCKET INVESTING

Throughout American preindustrial history, businesses generally operated with a one-pocket mindset, although such vocabulary did not exist at the time. Businesses tended to be family-owned while wholly involved in and contained by individual communities. Profit was sought as a means of subsistence, limited by gold-backed banking systems and a general lack of infrastructural connectivity, which prevented real scalability until the mid-nineteenth century. Between 1850 and 1980, the world became a more interconnected place with more advanced communication and transportation systems. When paired with the dramatic transformation in banking systems, this globalization created new avenues for economic growth. Furthermore, the associated creation of new profitability opportunities transformed the socioeconomic theory landscape.[3]

As sociology and economic study flourished in the late twentieth century, Milton Friedman famously published *Capitalism and Freedom*, which shaped modern definitions of capitalism for the next half-century and counting. A central tenet of Friedman's beliefs is that "there is one and only one social responsibility of business—to use its resources and engage in activities designed to increase its profits so long as it stays within the rules of the game, which is to say, engages in open and free competition without deception or fraud."[4]

Friedman made his bold claim in response to a growing number of businesspeople who argued that "business is not concerned 'merely' with profit but also with promoting desirable 'social' ends; that business has a 'social conscience' and takes seriously its responsibilities for providing employment, eliminating discrimination, avoiding pollution and whatever else."[5] To Friedman, this idea was the product of a reckless intellectual movement that put free society at risk.[6] His alternative solution isolated social responsibility from business activities, relying instead on moral individuals to pursue philanthropy through strictly charitable venues.

FAITH-BASED INITIATIVES AND NEGATIVE SCREENING PUSHBACK

While Friedman's approach has by now become so widely embraced that it feels like the way things have always been, his theory is relatively new. For centuries up to that point, entire faith groups advocated for a socially responsible approach to business and money management. Sharia law and *The Book of Discipline of the United Methodist Church* alike require people to integrate their faith values with their financial practices, in some cases explicitly stating what kinds of investment opportunities to pursue or avoid.[7] As Friedman championed bifurcating social activities from business activities, many religious denominations and organizations began to crystallize their position on socially responsible investing.

This pushback gained momentum in the 1980s during South African apartheid, when a significant number of individuals and organizations pulled their investments from companies with South African operations, citing their values-based concerns. The eighties also saw the creation of funds like the Calvert Social Investment Fund Balanced Portfolio and the Parnassus Fund, which used positive and negative screens to match the values of Methodists at the time, including issues like pollution and worker treatment.[8]

During the 1990s and 2000s, the idea of corporate social responsibility (CSR) emerged in response to highly publicized corruption cases like the Keating Five or Enron scandals. As CSR became the universal standard for business management, its rise was further backed by developed strategy and research showing the long-term capital benefits of socially responsible practices. Along with and emerging from CSR, environmental, social and governance investing (ESG) became an increasingly foundational approach to investing as a growing body of evidence pointed towards its greater return on investment over preceding investment approaches. Out of ESG grew practices like impact investing, values-based investing, and concessionary funding—which leads us to one pocket.

WHY ONE-POCKET INVESTING MATTERS TODAY

One-pocket investing represents the natural evolution of what has been a long and organic arc toward holistic economic participation. In its consideration of not only portfolio structure but also the complex and unique processes that surround investing, one-pocket investing is a holistic mindset more than just a strategy. As such, it's an accessible way of thinking, whether you just created your first digital wallet or you manage the investments of a Fortune 500 company.

The potential impact of embracing a one-pocket approach is enormous. The total value of all publicly listed companies in the world is around $200 trillion, while the total value of all charitable endowments in the world equals just over $1.5 trillion—only 5 percent of which is required to be actually dispersed into charitable activities.[9] If that disparity continues, a two-pocket mindset will prevent us from being able to solve or even mediate the humanitarian crises of our era. But if even a fraction of the world's companies and individuals adopt a one-pocket mindset, we could begin to make meaningful and sustainable changes in communities throughout the world.

The key is understanding that one pocket isn't just an approach to investing—it's a way of outwardly expressing our deeply held value systems. Moving beyond understanding money as a tool and toward understanding money as an expression of our core identity is what the one-pocket mindset is about.

ONE-POCKET VS. IMPACT INVESTING

A significant portion of the conversation around alternative approaches to investing uses the term "impact investing," along with "socially responsible investing," "values-based investing," and a handful of additional terms. These phrases have been more widely adopted into the investing lexicon than "one-pocket mindset," so it's worth asking what the value is in making a distinction. I believe that thinking of investments merely in fiscal terms doesn't capture the true depth and breadth of resource stewardship. The existing vocabulary limits what's possible by relying on the conceptual framework proposed by Friedman—by separating "investing" from "impact investing" and therefore implying it's possible to invest without having an impact.

On the contrary, all investment has an impact. "One pocket" captures this reality by acknowledging the unavoidable consequences of our approach to resource stewardship. It's not that impact investing or socially responsible investing are bad or unhelpful terms but that they reflect only a small facet of reality. In truth, we need a more holistic understanding of our economies that grasps the interconnected nature of individual, socially-minded, and capital-focused efforts. "One pocket" allows us to do just that.

ONE-POCKET VS. TWO-POCKET

Many investors are familiar with the values-based arguments for socially responsible investing. But often the financial opportunities present in impact investing come as a surprise. In fact, a Cambridge Associates report showed that impact investment funds garnered above-average returns in developed markets and significantly higher returns in developing markets.[10] The report emphasized that a thoughtful approach to creating an impact portfolio is key in determining investment success. Helpfully, the one-pocket mindset elevates the approach to be just as important as the actual portfolio, and as such lends itself to creating significant social and financial value.

Beyond financial returns, a growing number of individuals consider social responsibility an important priority. One study found that Millennial investors made more social-impact investments than any other investor segment, and 85 percent of Millennial investors "signaled interest for this type of investing."[11] That trend will only continue to grow as an awareness of the complex effects of our investments continues to shape norms and as younger generations develop an ever-stronger bent toward community and social responsibility. The one-pocket mindset offers a way of approaching economic engagement that doesn't require people to compromise their values to achieve their target returns or vice versa. More importantly, it actively cultivates a total engagement in values-driven work.

For organizations, one-pocket investing offers a way to integrate brand identity and values with social and fiscal responsibility. The same growing awareness that shapes individual investments extends to a growing awareness of the complex impact of business and organizational activities—and alongside awareness, accountability. Embracing the one-pocket mindset can allow companies to align all of their activities—social, economic, or otherwise—along a core set of values. Not only can this have a positive impact on brand image, but it can also have a real, positive impact on company value.[12]

A key factor in value growth stems from the fact that the one-pocket mindset expands the definition of who organizational stakeholders are. When Friedman talks about businesses focusing solely on profit "within the rules of the game," he thinks of enterprises as the only players. The reality is much more complex. A business cannot survive without productive employees, a functional economy, a healthy environment, a stable government, and a host of other entities. Likewise, these same entities benefit from strong businesses. One pocket allows us to view this as a clear stakeholder relationship that further integrates the context of our economic activities into our values-based decisions.

LOOKING THROUGH THE ONE-POCKET LENS

At some point, the one-pocket concept must become a to-do list, a plan. Otherwise we're left with just a dream of what could be. Fortunately, innovative thinkers in finance are paving the way with creative, pioneering one-pocket strategies that are already creating real change in communities from New York to Salt Lake City. And these strategies start with defining values.

If you want your resource management to align with your values, you have to understand what your values are in a specific, honest way. At the Caprock Group, Robert Kim works extensively to help families think through their values, and one of his priorities is communicating how much nuance any given issue contains. For example, individuals might be passionate about underprivileged youth and so want to invest in education opportunities. But, says Kim, "if you're in the shoes of those kids, it's not just education that matters. Your time with your parents matters, and if your parents are working four jobs, have no time for homework or anything else, that affects a child's well-being. So you have to think about creating job opportunities in that region." Kim's—and Caprock's—priority is to unravel the diverse factors impacting childhood well-being and how complex investment portfolios can become, even when centered around a single vision.

In addition to a values audit, you will need to audit your existing investments and business activities as well. Does their impact move the needle toward your vision? While the exact process is unique to every individual or organization, the same mindset of curiosity and questioning is just as important. As with auditing your values, expect to discover a complex and nuanced picture of your investment impact. In talking through issues that impact underprivileged youth, Kim explains that a primary challenge for rural families is climate change, which makes weather patterns harsher and more volatile. But determining how much your investments mitigate climate change can be impossibly complicated. For example, does investing in Walmart help or hurt rural families? Walmart regularly uses local suppliers, but they also create pollution with their massive store footprints and supply chain structure. The way that you answer such questions throughout the audit process will come to define your one-pocket mindset.

The process of answering difficult value questions begins with outlining your visionary and financial goals. How aggressive or conservative those goals are will guide the specific diversification of your one-pocket portfolio, which can in turn help you hone in on the bright lines of your values.

At the same time, creating benchmarks for your vision is important even if you know exactly what the values guiding that vision are. As with any investment, performance is measured by finding the difference between the goals you set and the actual outcomes of your portfolio. In the one-pocket approach, this includes not only financial return benchmarks but also social and environmental impact benchmarks. While ROI is a pretty straightforward goal to set, measuring social impact can be more challenging and often requires a bit of creativity. To return to our example of underprivileged youth, you may need to measure a whole set of metrics including changes in after-school program enrollment, rates of childhood illness, adult unemployment, and any number of other factors. Checking both these complex social metrics and financial ROI consistently will give you a clear picture of how your investments are driving your vision.

While the one-pocket mindset is primarily referenced within the context of investment, it's more than just an investment approach. As a mindset, it guides the whole picture of how resources should be stewarded, including time, access, and space. My expertise is within capital resources, but I've discovered that folks who embrace a one-pocket mindset soon manage all of the resources at their disposal in much more intentional ways. What that looks like for you or your organization will be completely unique to your vision, but my recommendation is to ask the same questions that guide your investment audit of your other resources.

In the end, the question that one pocket asks us can be a difficult one. It isn't "Are your resources invested well?" or even "How are you making a difference with what you've been given?" It is instead the question "Are your values important enough for you to align what you have and do in their service?" Our answers to that question will come to define not just us but also the trajectory of global change for generations to come.

CHAPTER 14

FOCUS ON ETERNITY

Casey Crawford

I'm not a good investor. Sorry, I just had to get that off my chest. It's important that you know where I'm coming from so that you can hear what I hope God would want for you.

I'm an entrepreneur at heart, which, in a way, means I share a lot of the same desires as many Faith Driven Investors. I'm passionate about solving the problems God has brought before me, both in my local community and around the world. And I'm dedicated to deploying capital toward those ends. Sometimes that looks like charitable giving. Other times it looks like investing capital. In both arenas, I seek to serve the Lord God and the vision he has given me for seeing his Kingdom come on earth as it is in heaven.

There used to be a time in my life when I thought that would be easy, or at least natural and normal. Turns out, serving God with money is anything but easy. In fact, if you are truly a Faith Driven Investor and you're going to step out in faith, seeking first the Kingdom of God with all that he's entrusted to you, you'd better get ready, because you're in for a fight. At least, that has been our story at Movement Mortgage.

Today, Movement Mortgage has nearly five thousand team members. We're funding over $30 billion in mortgages in the United States. That's amazing, but it's not where we started fourteen years ago. At that time, God had some deep and painful work to do on me.

ARGUING WITH GOD

My first career was in the NFL, where I got to be part of a Super Bowl championship team and experience all the hopes and dreams I had as a little boy. When that season of life ended, I prayed, "Lord, what's next? I want a life of impact. How should I do it?"

That seemed like the right prayer for someone who had been a follower of Jesus their whole life. But while my faith was sincere, there were parts of my life—and parts of my heart in particular—that the Lord needed to convict me on in order to prepare me for the work ahead.

This heart change started in 2007 when we had the opportunity to open a mortgage company. People generally remember that this was the Great Recession, but you might not remember how bad, how deep, and how scary a time it was. I was in Charlotte, North Carolina, otherwise known as the first city built on banking. We watched Bank of America and Wachovia teeter on the brink of failure. IndyMac was gone. Bear Stearns was gone. And Lehman Brothers had failed. The entire world financial network was crumbling. And at the epicenter of the evil and greed that caused that collapse sat the US mortgage market. This is the part of the story I felt God had called me into.

At the same time as I was processing all of this, I served on a church elder board that was going through a really tough time. In the middle of the financial crisis, the church was running out of money, which meant late-night meetings looking over the budget, trying to figure out where to cut back and save.

As those conversations unfolded, we realized we were going to need to cut people's salaries in order to survive. Obviously, that was an unpopular decision. Looking back, I may have handled the conversation a little differently today, but at the time, as I was the only business guy in the meeting, it became a mathematical problem. Here's how much money we have as a church. Here's how long we have until we're out. Here's how we can extend that date, and so on and so forth.

It was a really difficult, emotionally charged conversation. While we were working with our church to process these difficult financial decisions, I was also praying and seeking the Lord to ask him if he would call me to start a mortgage bank as a response to this crisis.

As I was on the way out of town to have a day of prayer and meditation about starting a mortgage company, all I could think about was how unbelievable the situation at our church was. It shocked me that these pastors were so tied up in money and having such a hard time making a tough call. In my head, I was having arguments, bashing their hypocritical sin, and blaming them for not having a Kingdom-focused mindset.

And in that moment, God hit me with a right hook to the jaw.

I don't know that I can say I've heard from God many times in my life, but this was the most explicit his voice has ever sounded in my ears. All I heard him say was "What makes you think you're so different?" I stopped for a second . . . then had the exact opposite response anyone should ever have in this situation. I started arguing with God.

The excuses poured out. *No, you don't understand. I'm an entrepreneur, and those guys are called into ministry. It's two totally different things. I'm supposed to be about making money, but they're supposed to be focused on serving the church. Oh, and by the way, God, I've always tithed, even quite generously at times.* And on and on, I wrestled with God all weekend.

At the end of my time of solitude, I realized God was

calling me to start a mortgage company. But the truth is, he did more than call me. He convicted me. He essentially said, "Casey, look while you're paying lip service to this all being about me. You say you want to be a Faith Driven Entrepreneur and build something for me, but this is actually all about you. It's about your kingdom, not mine." God pointed out this false humility that I hadn't realized was there. It was like I was pseudo-giving God the glory, but really it was all about me. That realization was brutal, but it changed the way I viewed money forever.

MORE THAN JUST A TITHE

Having grown up in the church, all I really knew was that you should tithe. It was my understanding that if you're a good Christian, that's what you do. I had done that my whole life—I had been the "good Christian"—but it didn't negate what God had brought to my attention. I knew he was still right. I knew I was building my own kingdom, not his.

What I felt challenged to do then, returning home after this conversation with God, was to ask a different question. Instead of *How much can I make?* I started asking, *How much is enough?* because I really felt that I needed to hold myself to the same standards I had asked these pastors to abide by. So the question then became, *How much do I really need to take care of my family, and how can I faithfully use the rest for God's Kingdom?*

Through prayer and the counsel of friends and family, we decided to come up with a salary cap. People like Alan Barnhart and Pete Ochs were inspirational as I looked to change my mindset from how much money can I keep to how much can I give away.

I wish I could tell you I just flipped the switch and immediately became a faithful steward of God's resources, but I didn't. I often find that I have more in common with Jacob wrestling with God than I do with Peter getting out of the boat to follow Jesus. I wanted to make money. I wanted to build a successful business. But I wanted to do all that for *me*. It wasn't easy to let go of the selfish side of these desires and hand them entirely over to God.

Of course, this shouldn't be a surprise to any of us who read Scripture. We know the number of times that God warns us about this. For entrepreneurs and investors, this is one of the most difficult temptations we face because we're fundamentally in the business of making money. We're in the business of *business*. But over time, God helped me unclench my fists around these ideas of success and instead invited me to be faithful with what he gave me.

With this mindset, we set forth to build a business that in every way was going to honor God and grow his Kingdom, not ours. But how? How do we do something like this? I love where Jesus answers the lawyer who asks him, "Hey, Lord, what's the most important commandment?" They wanted to get straight to the point. I can relate. And Jesus, of course, said there are two. We all know this: "'Love the Lord your God with all your heart and with all your soul and with all your mind and with all your strength.' The second is this: 'Love your neighbor as yourself.' There is no commandment greater than these."[1]

Well, we figured that if Jesus summarized the whole of the law into two really fundamental verses, couldn't that be a good mission statement for our company? So our mission statement is that we exist to love and value people by leading a movement of change in our industry, in corporate cultures, and in communities across America.

For us, the mission had to be about others. It wasn't about the projects we owned. It was about the people we served. In practice, that looks like taking the profits and investing them into his work to love the marginalized in the cities and communities that we're part of so that God will get the glory for all he's done in and through the business.

And while that's a fun and engaging vision to have, it took a lot of time to discern the how behind it all. We spent a great deal of time early on fasting, praying, and really seeking the Lord. All we asked was, "How is it that you would call us to steward these incredible resources that you're entrusting to us?" That's it. We knew what we had didn't belong to us, and we wanted the owner's advice on what to do with it. So we went to God.

INVESTING WITH AN ENTREPRENEURIAL MINDSET

Of course, that's a prayer God answered. As God allowed Movement to be more and more successful, we had excess cash that we could invest in the business but also in our community. We took the same approach to investing as we did with building Movement. We knew what was broken in the market, and we used entrepreneurial creativity to fix it. Now, we felt God calling us to do the same in our communities. When we opened up our hands and said to God, "This is your business; do with it as you will," he reminded us that he has always been in control by opening doors we never could've imagined.

The start of that happened when we learned how Christian schools that had set out to serve the urban poor failed over and over and over again. The reason researchers say they fail is kind of obvious: they run out of money. The donors dry up. It becomes a fundraising cycle, and they fail to fundamentally support themselves. It works fine in the wealthy suburbs, but Christian schools fail to serve the urban poor consistently and over a long period of time.

At the same time, we were also introduced to public charter schools. What we learned is that if a faith-based not-for-profit buys a piece of real estate, it can lease that building to a public charter school. Now, from 8:00 to 3:00, you teach secular, state-approved, federally approved curriculum. But the beauty is that before school, after school, and on weekends, that faith-based not-for-profit can utilize that building for Christ-centered, redemptive services—for the kids, the families, and that entire community.

We've watched God step into this business model and do incredible things. Over 75 percent of the children at these schools were at or below the poverty line, and they're having over 200 percent better academic success than their demographic peers. Not only that, but the schools are also generating a profit, which means we get to watch God do more and more and more. Now, we're going to individual government officials and saying that we will invest $100 million in your state in the next three years to build schools for the poorest kids. Our ask is that if we double the academic results of these children, then we want ninety cents on the dollar of what the states are giving traditional public schools. Basically, we're offering a 10 percent discount for 200 percent better academic results.

Often people look at what we're doing and call us generous. That's not so much generosity as it is a wise use of capital. The reality is that we're profoundly selfish. When we move resources toward what we see God doing in the world, we experience joy. I want more of that. Good investors invest in pattern recognition, right? That's what we're doing. We see God move, so we move toward him. Then we get to experience what he's doing, so we follow him wherever he will take us next.

Now, it sounds simple, but the truth is this only happens through prayer, fasting, and reading Scripture. Entrepreneurs love to move quickly, and that often helps us in the end. But if we know anything from Saul and the other Old Testament kings, anytime we move before we've communicated with God, we're probably going the wrong way. I would challenge you then, Faith Driven Investor, to ask God where he would have you go. He wants to invite you to experience the work he's doing in the world. I'm sure of it. And as someone who is watching his work happen in real time, let me be the first to tell you, it is amazing.

One of the greatest lies that pervades the Christian investing world is that while you could do a little for the Kingdom today, if you wait and invest shrewdly for a while, you'll be able to do a lot tomorrow. The problem is that God hasn't promised us tomorrow. In fact, just the opposite! He warns us that the days are evil and that Jesus' second coming will arrive like a thief in the night. We're so focused on compounding our interest that we miss the chance to compound our impact.

WHAT WILL YOU DO?

We might have several ready-made answers about the ways *we're* growing our investments, the markets *we're* beginning to enter, the big plans for expansion and funding and hiring new people and on and on. But here's the gut-wrencher—are we working for our return or for God's return?

I know that the Parable of the Talents is a regularly discussed passage for Faith Driven Investors, but let me put forward one simple thought I see from this story: action isn't optional. See, some of the servants in the Parable of the Talents did what they were supposed to do. They knew the master was coming back, so they worked hard to give him a large dividend upon his return. But one didn't. One servant sat on the money, hoarding it and hiding it, probably dreading the day the master would return or secretly hoping that day might never come.

The thing is, there's a city to come. God has told us he will return and bring heaven to earth. In the meantime, sitting on our hands and waiting for that day isn't good enough. We have the opportunity to work in a way that prepares our companies, our cities, and our hearts for God's eventual arrival.

This actually isn't a lesson on working harder so we'll have more success to show God. It's about seeing our work as an act of service to the Master. It's about understanding that he has given us something, namely a business or an investment portfolio, with which we can honor, glorify, and worship him. Don't bury what God has given you. That's not just a command from Scripture. It's an invitation to do what God wants you to do so that you can continue to experience more of him in your life.

The servants who used what the master gave them got something much greater than a financial return—they had the satisfaction of giving it back to the master. We are like children creating a drawing that God will hang on his refrigerator. He wants to be proud of how we've worked for him.

He wants to look at us with a smile and say, "Well done, my good and faithful servant." God actually wants that for us. So, what will we do today to work for his return? Will we struggle to possess and hoard what we've been given? Or will we fight the daily battle to submit ourselves to the role of stewarding and surrendering our businesses to the God who already owns it all?

I hope that you invest in Kingdom-minded businesses and experience great returns. I hope that you continue to effectively deploy capital in highly leveraged ways to accomplish godly outcomes. That would be fantastic. But what I wish the most is that you would close this book and accept the call that Jesus has placed on your life to experience his presence in and through the investments you make.

If you choose to follow God in the way you give, save, spend, invest, and steward the money he has put under your control, I can't promise you'll experience positive ROI year after year. Your money might not grow. Seriously. But I can promise you an eternal ROI that's better than anything this world can offer. I can promise you the experience of working alongside our Creator, our God in heaven.

In my life, I've experienced a smidgen of what God is doing. I've seen only glimpses. But those times have changed my life. God is at work around the world. God is at work in your community. The first step is to pray, and the second step is to go. So, do it.

Do something.

SEEK WISE COUNSEL

Ron Blue and Rob West

Money is confusing. It's like a puzzle with a lot of different pieces. How you put the money puzzle together and what goes where are questions that people spend their lives trying to answer. And it's important. Billy Graham often remarked that if somebody gets their money right, most of the rest of their life works out. The way we view our money matters. This idea is where this book started, and it's only fitting that we end here too.

How we *think about* money impacts how we *act with* money. Our beliefs determine our behavior. If our thoughts about money are based on biblical truth, then we'll better understand how to make the best decisions with money.

Often what people ask financial advisors is this: "How am I doing?" Everybody, whether wealthy or poor, wants to know how they're doing. And the answer to that question is always unique. Different families, different life stages, and different experiences all necessitate their own unique answers. And providing those answers takes not only a great deal of expertise but also a tremendous amount of wisdom. If we aren't drawing on God's wisdom to answer that question, then we won't get to the right answer.

The Bible has 2,350 verses that deal with money. Two-thirds of Jesus' parables discuss money in one way or another. And there's more said about money in the Bible than about heaven and hell combined. We can be certain that God cares about how we use money. Money decisions are spiritual decisions.

Think of it like this. God has given us resources and responsibilities, and the way we value, prioritize, and respond to those things reflects the way we view the one who gave them to us. Often our checkbooks are a better reflection of our spiritual beliefs than anything we might say or do in church.

John Steinbeck once wrote a letter to Adlai Stevenson in 1959 that said this: "A strange species we are. We can stand anything God and nature can throw at us save only plenty. If I wanted to destroy a nation, I would give it too much and would have it on its knees, miserable, greedy and sick."[1] We don't often hear sermons on greed anymore, but it's an idea that's found throughout Scripture. One place is a parable that may not immediately jump out at you as one about greed.

When Jesus told the Parable of the Soils, it's unclear whether the crowd understood what he was saying. His disciples certainly didn't, so later they asked him. And this is Jesus' response:

> This is the meaning of the parable: The seed is the word of God. Those along the path are the ones who hear, and then the devil comes and takes away the word from their hearts, so that they may not believe and be saved. Those on the rocky ground are the ones who receive the word with joy when they hear it, but they have no root. They believe for a while, but in the time of testing they fall away. The seed that fell among thorns stands for those who hear, but as they go on their way they are choked by *life's worries, riches and pleasures*, and they do not mature. But the seed on good soil stands for those with a noble and good heart, who hear the word, retain it, and by persevering produce a crop.
>
> LUKE 8:11-15, EMPHASIS ADDED

Life's worries, riches, and pleasures. That's what John Steinbeck was talking about. Now, we don't know if he was a believer, but he clearly understood a principle that Jesus tried to explain to his disciples. The devil is capable of preventing the good seed from taking root, and so also are worries and riches and the pleasures of this life.

The bottom line is simple: you can serve either God or money, but not both. The Bible makes that clear, as Andy Crouch mentioned in his chapter earlier. That's the choice you're going to be confronted with. You're going to hear three thousand advertisements a day telling you that money will solve all your problems. Those are the thornbushes Jesus described. But let's not ignore the end of that passage. Not every seed is choked. Some persist and bear fruit because of the good soil they land in.

FAITH DRIVEN INVESTING AND GIVING GROUPS

So, what will increase your chances of finding yourself in good soil and thus bearing fruit? Well, the key is education and community.

You just finished reading a book about how your faith influences the way you invest, and you may be asking yourself, *What now?* It's hard to figure out the next steps alone. Thankfully, there are resources available that make the process of taking your next step (or your first step) a little bit easier. For starters, a Faith Driven Investing group is a great way to find like-minded men and women who are on this same journey with you. They're asking the same questions you are, wrestling through the same issues, and can be an excellent resource to remind you that you are not alone.

It's always better to live in community, so finding a group—either through the Faith Driven Investor ministry or through your local church—can go a long way.

Over the past year, these groups of entrepreneurs and investors have met online or in-person with people from over eighty-eight different countries. There's no cost or catch. It's just a group of believers who connect over teaching and stories that might inspire conversations to spur one another on to know God more fully through the way we steward what he has entrusted to us.

Maybe you're looking for a group of like-minded investors who will rally around redeeming different parts of your city, or maybe you feel called to invest in other areas of the world, addressing complex problems. You can go further together. You can learn more at the faithdriveninvestor.org website.

Then, once you've found a team, it helps to have a coach. That's where financial advisors can come in.

THE CERTIFIED KINGDOM ADVISOR

Life is better lived in community, and finding your tribe can go a long way. Of course, there are some questions that are too complex or too personal for a group of friends to answer.

That's where a Certified Kingdom Advisor (CKA) professional will help.

Every individual seeking a financial advisor in any discipline looks for someone who is competent, performs their work with excellence, demonstrates humility and integrity, and seeks to advance the client's interests first and foremost. Many advisors, whether a CKA or not, can meet these requirements. So, what's the difference?

An advisor who shares a biblical worldview and an eternal perspective can provide tremendous value as you seek to wisely manage the resources God has placed in your hands.

One of the foundational principles of the coursework to become a CKA is that God owns it all and we are merely his stewards. Acknowledging that our wealth doesn't belong to us but to him can provide wonderful clarity and perspective from which to make decisions about how to give, save, spend, and invest. Furthermore, an advisor who is a believer in Jesus Christ is undergoing constant transformation by the Holy Spirit and can be held to a higher standard of character and integrity.

As we noted earlier, the answer to the question "how am I doing?" is different for everyone. We can have great giving opportunities, ideas, aspirations, intentions, and a lot of things, but we need to boil those down into the context of where we are, what we're doing, and how we want to be doing.

That's where advisors can come in. They bring a holistic approach to your finances to say you're doing okay or not or that you need to change this or keep doing that. Faith Driven Investing is desirable and legitimate, but it needs to fit into the context of how you want to be using your financial assets.

A CKA is an advisor who has been trained from a biblical worldview, has met an experience requirement, and has committed to be a person of character, who serves you with financial advice on how to best meet the goals God has given you with his resources. Some CKA professionals pursue a faith-based investing specialty, meaning they offer financial plans and investments based on the client's personal convictions, avoiding investments in certain companies and embracing investments in others. This can be done through publicly traded investments (stocks, mutual funds, ETFs, etc.) for investors of all account sizes. And, for those investors who meet certain income or net worth requirements, privately held investments can offer the potential for even greater Kingdom impact. (If you'd like to learn more, visit kingdomadvisors.com.)

Faith Driven Investing is the practice of expressing your personal convictions through your investment decisions by determining how you can put your money into places and things that are having an impact. These opportunities exist. You just have to find them and have the willingness to do exactly what God is prompting you to do.

This isn't a journey you have to travel alone. Find your tribe, connect with a like-minded advisor, and choose to be vulnerable and transparent with the people who can help you go where God is calling you. Accountability is the annoying little secret of success. And the Kingdom advances through relationships.

Whether you work with a CKA or join a Faith Driven Investor group, know that God is in the business of working through his people. Surround yourself with those who share your heart and passion to see his work accomplished in the world, and know that every investment you make can and will have an impact.

NOTES

CHAPTER 1: IDENTIFIED IN CHRIST

1. Iain Hamish Murray, *David Martyn Lloyd-Jones: The Fight of Faith, 1939–1981* (Edinburgh: Banner of Truth Trust, 1990), 335.
2. Benjamin Nugent, "Draft; Upside of Distraction," *New York Times*, February 3, 2013, https://archive.nytimes.com/query.nytimes.com/gst/fullpage-9802E5DC1F3AF930A35751C0A9659D8B63.html.

CHAPTER 2: THE SERVANT OF ONE MASTER

1. See Deuteronomy 7:9.

CHAPTER 3: ATTUNED TO GOD'S WORD

1. See John 10:10.
2. See Ephesians 6:10-17.
3. See Romans 12:2.
4. See John 10:10.

CHAPTER 4: AWARE OF THE POWER OF MONEY AND MARKETS

1. Daniel Defoe, introduction to *An Essay upon Projects*, ed. Henry Morley (London: Cassell & Company, Limited, 1887), https://www.gutenberg.org/files/4087/4087-h/4087-h.htm.
2. Defoe, *An Essay upon Projects*.
3. Adele Simmons, "Outside Opinion: Skeptics Were Wrong; South Africa Divestment Worked," *Chicago Tribune*, December 15, 2013, https://www.chicagotribune.com/business/ct-xpm-2013-12-15-ct-biz-1215-outside-opinion-20131215-story.html.
4. Simmons, "Outside Opinion."

CHAPTER 5: KNOWN FOR WHAT THEY'RE FOR

1. See, for example, N. T. Wright, *Surprised by Hope: Rethinking Heaven, the Resurrection, and the Mission of the Church* (New York: HarperCollins, 2008).
2. "Our Mission," 410 Medical, accessed April 28, 2022, https://410medical .com/410-medical/.

CHAPTER 6: REFLECTING CREATION BY MAKING NEW THINGS

1. "Big Ideas 2022," ARK Invest, accessed April 19, 2022, https://ark-invest .com/big-ideas-2022/.

CHAPTER 9: THINK DIFFERENTLY ABOUT RISK

1. See James 4:17.

CHAPTER 10: SEEK COLLABORATIVE COMMUNITY

1. See James 5:16.

CHAPTER 11: WORK LOCALLY AND GLOBALLY

1. Matthew 9:12-13.
2. United Nations, Department of Economic and Social Affairs, Population Division, *Population 2030: Demographic Challenges and Opportunities for Sustainable Development Planning (ST/ESA/SER.A/389)*, 2015, https:// www.un.org/en/development/desa/population/publications/pdf/trends /Population2030.pdf.
3. Matthew 22:36.

CHAPTER 13: PULL FROM ONE POCKET

1. William Donovan, "The Origins of Socially Responsible Investing," The Balance, January 31, 2022, https://www.thebalance.com/a-short-history -of-socially-responsible-investing-3025578.
2. Ross Baird, *The Innovation Blind Spot: Why We Back the Wrong Ideas and What to Do about It* (Dallas, TX: BenBella Books, 2017).
3. Alfred D. Chandler Jr., *The Visible Hand: The Managerial Revolution in American Business* (Cambridge, MA: Belknap Press, 2002).
4. Milton Friedman, "A Friedman Doctrine—The Social Responsibility of Business Is to Increase Its Profits," *New York Times*, September 13, 1970, https://www.nytimes.com/1970/09/13/archives/a-friedman-doctrine-the -social-responsibility-of-business-is-to.html#.
5. Friedman, "A Friedman Doctrine."
6. Friedman, "A Friedman Doctrine."
7. See *The Book of Discipline of the United Methodist Church* (Nashville: The

United Methodist Publishing House, 2016), https://www.cokesbury.
com/book-of-discipline-book-of-resolutions-free-versions; Mujtaba
Wani, "Sharia-Compliance and Sustainability," *Journal of Environmental
Investing—Working Paper*, March 10, 2015, https://www.google.com
/url?sa=t&rct=j&q=&esrc=s&source=web&cd=&ved=2ahUKEwj-yeXb6qv
3AhVjiOAKHSp9AgAQFnoECBUQAQ&url=http%3A%2F%2Fwww
.thejei.com%2Fwp-content%2Fuploads%2F2015%2F03%2FJEI-Working
-Paper-3-Sharia-compliance-and-Sustainability-Mujtaba-Wani-March-2015
.docx&usg=AOvVaw2ahuaaLZK7tLqt6bvJsR0d.

8. William Donovan, "The Origins of Socially Responsible Investing," The
   Balance, January 31, 2022, https://www.thebalance.com/a-short-history-of
   -socially-responsible-investing-3025578.

9. Charles McGrath, "Global Foundation Assets Reach $1.5 Trillion,"
   Pensions & Investments, May 8, 2018, https://www.pionline.com/article
   /20180508/INTERACTIVE/180509883/global-foundation-assets-reach
   -1-5-trillion.

10. "Introducing the Impact Investing Benchmark," Cambridge Associates,
    June 2015, https://thegiin.org/assets/documents/pub/Introducing_the
    _Impact_Investing_Benchmark.pdf.

11. Sarah Landrum, "Why Millennials Care about Social Impact Investing,"
    Forbes, November 4, 2016, https://www.forbes.com/sites/sarahlandrum
    /2016/11/04/why-millennials-care-about-social-impact-investing/?sh
    =685e179159c0.

12. Baird, *Innovation Blind Spot*.

CHAPTER 14: FOCUS ON ETERNITY

1. Mark 12:30-31.

AFTERWORD: SEEK WISE COUNSEL

1. John Steinbeck to Adlai Stevenson, 1959, quoted at "John Steinbeck's
   Letter—'A Morally Bankrupt Turn of Events,'" Writers Write, https://www
   .writerswrite.co.za/john-steinbeck-a-morally-bankrupt-turn-of-events/.

ABOUT THE AUTHORS

Henry Kaestner

Henry Kaestner cofounded the Faith Driven Entrepreneur, Investor, and Giving ministries, where he seeks to serve faith driven investors, funds, partners, advisors, and entrepreneurs through content and community. He is also a cofounder and partner at Sovereign's Capital, a private equity and venture capital management company, and previously cofounded Bandwidth (BAND), a Nasdaq-traded telecom company based in Raleigh, North Carolina.

Timothy Keller

Timothy Keller is the founding pastor of Redeemer Presbyterian Church in Manhattan, which he started in 1989 with his wife, Kathy, and three young sons. He is also the chairman and cofounder of Redeemer City to City (CTC), which starts new churches in New York and other global cities, and publishes books and resources for ministries in an urban environment.

Andy Crouch

Andy Crouch is partner for theology and culture at Praxis, an organization that works as a creative engine for redemptive entrepreneurship. He's also the author of *The Life We're Looking For*, *The Tech-Wise Family*, *Strong and Weak*, *Playing God*, and *Culture Making*.

Obie McKenzie

Prior to his retirement in 2018, Obie McKenzie was managing director at BlackRock Financial, the largest institutional asset management firm in the United States. He is an accomplished public speaker and has been an expository Bible teacher for over thirty years, first as senior Bible teacher at Canaan Baptist Church in Harlem, New York, and now at Community Baptist Church of Englewood, New Jersey.

Finny Kuruvilla

Finny Kuruvilla serves as the CIO for Eventide Funds, lead portfolio manager on the Eventide Gilead Fund, and portfolio manager on the Eventide Healthcare and Life Sciences Fund. He holds an MD from Harvard Medical School, a PhD in chemistry and chemical biology from Harvard University, a master's degree in electrical engineering and computer science from MIT, and a bachelor's degree from Caltech in chemistry.

Luke Roush

Luke Roush cofounded Sovereign's Capital in 2012 and is a managing partner in the firm. Prior to Sovereign's Capital, Luke had twelve years of experience in global commercialization and business development at both venture-backed and Fortune 500 companies. He also cofounded 410 Medical, a medical device company focused on pediatric trauma.

Cathie Wood

Cathie Wood is the founder and CIO/CEO of ARK Invest. With over forty years of experience identifying and investing in innovation, Cathie founded ARK to focus solely on disruptive innovation while adding new dimensions to research.

Greg Lernihan

Greg Lernihan is cofounder of Convergint Technologies. Started in a basement in 2001, Convergint is now the world's largest privately held electronic security firm with over 2,400 colleagues globally. He currently dedicates his time to mentoring budding entrepreneurs, investing in impact-related companies, and supporting Christian ministries passionately serving all parts of the world.

John and Ashely Marsh

Over the last twenty-five years, John and Ashely Marsh have guided over forty startup businesses in various industries,

---

such as construction, real estate investing, advertising, and also multiple restaurants. Together, they have renovated over 220 buildings within ten blocks of downtown Opelika, and now they steward over $1 billion in redemptive real estate in nine small towns (with populations of 800 to 180,000) around America through Marsh Collective.

Will Thomas

Will Thomas has been investing in organizations that demonstrate social and spiritual impact since 2013. Additionally, Will serves on the board of two publicly traded companies and as chairman of the board of Marketplace Chaplains. Previously, he was vice president at Capital Southwest Corporation, where he made investments in private companies and provided advice.

Efosa Ojomo

Efosa Ojomo leads the global prosperity research group at the Clayton Christensen Institute for Disruptive Innovation, a think tank based in Boston and Silicon Valley. His work has been published and covered by the *Wall Street Journal*, *Harvard Business Review*, the *Guardian*, *Quartz*, *Forbes*, *Fortune*, The World Bank, NPR, and several other media outlets.

Richard Okello

Richard Okello is a cofounder and partner at Sango Capital. Prior to cofounding Sango, Richard was a principal at

Makena Capital, a large private endowment. At Makena, he managed portfolios with substantial emerging markets exposure and reviewed and critiqued hundreds of investment opportunities, ultimately investing over $15 billion into over 300 funds and co-investments across all major public and private asset classes globally.

Jessica Kim

Jessica Kim is the cofounder and CEO of ianacare, on a mission to encourage, empower, and equip family caregivers as they navigate care at home. Previously, at the age of nineteen, she started Jessica's Wonders, a baked goods company, out of her college dorm room. She raised $1 million her senior year (with braces) and grew the company to national distribution.

Bryce Butler

Bryce Butler is the managing director of Access Ventures. Prior to starting Access Ventures, he was the executive director of the BlueSky Network, a venture philanthropy family office in southern Indiana with activities around the world in microfinance, clean energy, sustainable agriculture, mobile payments, and entrepreneurship/innovation.

Casey Crawford

In addition to being an NFL Super Bowl champion, Casey Crawford is the founder and CEO of Movement, a multi-billion-dollar mortgage company. He is also a sought-after media guest whose appearances span CNBC's "Squawk Box," Bloomberg, and Fox News with print features in the *Wall Street Journal* and *TIME* magazine.

Ron Blue

In 1970, Ron Blue founded an Indianapolis-based CPA firm that has grown to be one of the fifty largest CPA firms in the United States. After leaving the CPA firm in 1977, Ron became administrative vice president of Leadership Dynamics International. He then retired from the financial planning firm in 2003 in order to lead Kingdom Advisors, an international effort to equip and motivate Christian financial professionals to serve the body of Christ by implementing biblical wisdom in their lives and practices. Ron is also the author of seventeen books on personal finance from a biblical perspective.

Rob West

Rob West is the president of Kingdom Advisors, a professional association promoting the integration of a biblical worldview into financial practices. Rob is also the host of the popular radio and podcast series *Moneywise*, one of the leading sources for education and training for Christian advisors and investors.

FAITH DRI>EN
INVESTOR

Investing can be a lonely journey . . .
But it doesn't have to be.

Join a small group of other investors meeting weekly or monthly and wrestling with what it means to be a Faith Driven Investor.

DON'T GO IT ALONE

The investing journey is often a lonely one. But it doesn't have to be that way. Faith Driven Investor has designed an eight week video study that you can walk through with a community of investors.

Together, we'll watch videos that feature teaching from leaders like Tim Keller, Andy Crouch, as well as real-life stories of investors living these lessons out. These small groups are for anyone looking to be good stewards of the resources they've been entrusted with and connect in like-minded community.

Join a group at https://www.faithdriveninvestor.org/watch-with-a-group.

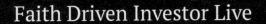

FAITH DRI>EN
INVESTOR

Faith Driven Investor Live

Think of the one-day virtual conference as a family reunion for the movement streaming to 100+ Watch Parties across the globe to hear from others on the journey and be reminded that you are not alone.

FIND YOUR PLACE

Faith Driven Investor hosts regular events that give you a chance to connect with other investors, learn from those who have been in your shoes, and grow from the counsel and wisdom of others who have experienced every form of success (and failure) you can imagine.

Whether you want to participate in our regular Faith Driven Investor Groups or the annual conference, there's a place for you. No matter what phase of the journey you're on, you can find somewhere to meet, connect, grow, and learn.

Find out more about the annual conference at faithdriveninvestorlive.org.

FAITH DRI>EN
INVESTOR

Marketplace

Connecting You to Stories
of Faith Driven Funds
and Entrepreneurs

FAITH DRIVEN FUNDS AND ENTREPRENEURS

Are you a Faith Driven Investor looking for funds and entrepreneurs that
share your vision? Marketplace is where faith aligned capital intersects with
faith driven leaders. It's where every investment has an impact.

Some of the leading family offices, accredited investors, and private equity
groups of the Faith Driven Movement share their story. You can view the
stories of funds and entrepreneurs from around the world, and put capital
to work. Whether you're looking for opportunities or the chance to connect
with other like-minded investors, this is a great fit to learn about the
movement.

To get access to Marketplace, visit faithdriveninvestor.org/marketplace.